D0938465

THE MAN WHO WOULD STOP AT NOTHING

Also by Melissa Holbrook Pierson

*Dark Horses and Black Beauties*
*The Perfect Vehicle*
*The Place You Love Is Gone*

# THE MAN
# WHO WOULD STOP
# AT NOTHING

## Long-Distance
## Motorcycling's
## Endless Road

### Melissa Holbrook Pierson

W. W. NORTON & COMPANY · NEW YORK LONDON

Copyright © 2011 by Melissa Holbrook Pierson

All rights reserved
Printed in the United States of America
First Edition

For information about permission to reproduce selections from this book,
write to Permissions, W. W. Norton & Company, Inc.,
500 Fifth Avenue, New York, NY 10110

For information about special discounts for bulk purchases, please contact W. W. Norton Special Sales at specialsales@wwnorton.com or
800-233-4830

Manufacturing by Courier Westford
Book design by Dana Sloan
Production manager: Anna Oler

Library of Congress Cataloging-in-Publication Data

Pierson, Melissa Holbrook.
The man who would stop at nothing : long-distance motorcycling's endless
road / Melissa Holbrook Pierson.
    p. cm.
ISBN 978-0-393-07904-3 (hardcover)
1. Ryan, John C. 2. Motorcyclists—United States—Biography.
3. Motorcycling—United States. 4. Endurance sports—United States.
5. Iron Butt Rally. I. Title.
GV1060.2.R93P54 2011
796.75092—dc23
[B]
                                        2011026188


W. W. Norton & Company, Inc.
500 Fifth Avenue, New York, N.Y. 10110
www.wwnorton.com

W. W. Norton & Company Ltd.
Castle House, 75/76 Wells Street, London W1T 3QT

1 2 3 4 5 6 7 8 9 0

To Raphael
*heart of my heart*

# Contents

# Foreword: *Forward*

**THE RIDE IS OUT THERE** waiting, invisible, and goes on (and on) without us. It begins with an ancient idea in the minds of men. They are consumed with the desire to go somewhere. The distances through which they move are measured against the body and the time it takes to get there. The miles begin with the mile.

The word comes from *mille passuum*, a measure of one thousand paces. (The Romans used the foot pace only because the motorcycle had not yet been invented.) And, since we are who we are, together yet individual, variable yet similar, there is the Scots mile (5,920 feet), the Irish mile (6,720 feet), the "old English" mile, the metric mile. Also the Danish *mil*, the German *Meile*. We are a law-passing animal, though, as well as a movement-desiring one, so in 1592 an Act of Parliament codified the statute mile, and there it rests, at 5,280 feet.

*He seems miles away.*
*I'd go a country mile for you.*
*That was a milestone for me.*
*Give that kid an inch and she'll take a mile.*

Necessarily, as distance is indissoluble from time in the vast limits of human experience, the word is also used to refer to "a vague measure of time" (as put by the *Oxford English Dictionary*, the compendium housing the words we have devised to express all that experience). *I will see you in a few miles,* I said, not knowing what I meant. Then I started down a road, away from you.

. . .

*I missed it by a mile.*

. . .

**IT IS INDEED** a vague measure of time. In my case, the pointless wandering comprised an eleven-year sleep of motorcyclelessness. When I woke, I was in a dark hallway, stumbling forward with hopeful hands held out. Then I saw a slice of light. Closer, and I could see the title on the door from under which it spilled: *Bikes Here. Enter and Be Saved.* Inside was such strangeness: Everything has changed! At least on the surface—the great increase of riders, numbered in hundreds of thousands; the armored gear; the digitized, the carbon-fibered, the ABSed and GPSed, the piled-up complications of parts and pumps and suspensions; the listservs and forums ever-blossoming to encompass billions of words and countless thousands of clever avatars behind which masks were people who rode faster and braked better and knew more about more minutiae than was ever conceived of a decade earlier. I reeled back. For a moment. Then, in the very center of the swirling din, I saw that what was elemental had not changed. For it never could. The joy. The need. The familial bond of blood. The erotics of risk.

Finally, the realization that this all begins with miles. And the consumption thereof.

# 1. A damnably labyrinthine branch

*For some men, nothing is written unless they write it themselves.*

—SHERIF ALI ON T. E. LAWRENCE IN *LAWRENCE OF ARABIA*

*Tommy Barban was a ruler, Tommy was a hero. . . . As a rule, he drank little; courage was his game. . . . Recently an eighth of the area of his skull had been removed by a Warsaw surgeon and was knitting under his hair, and the weakest person in the café could have killed him with a flip of a knotted napkin.*

—F. SCOTT FITZGERALD, *TENDER IS THE NIGHT*

**DETERMINATION IN THE FORM** of a man walks toward you. A metaphor about human transcendence made real and clothed in one hell of a suit. It's a green Roadcrafter. No, a gray one. No, some other color, one the Aerostich company doesn't sell: the color of miles, thousands of them, with their attendant filth built up in layer after layer that could never be washed clean. Nor would he want that; this, along with the scrapes and tiny tears and the shape of the well-made body underneath molded into the Gore-Tex so that now it could probably stand up by itself like a knight's full armor in the Met's medieval wing, prove the visible badge of something otherwise hidden, the soul of the long-distance endurance rider.

This particular one, John Charles Ryan, a bit over six foot two and forty-eight years old, has a dry sense of humor, evidenced by something else on the suit, so that together it and the motorcycle he rides display all you need to know, at least initially. Just above the heart is sewn a patch bearing the NASA logo. It both is and is not a joke. Later you will have to wonder if in fact he is not rocket-propelled.

It is January 2008. New York City. The annual commercial motorcycle show. The day's temperature is to top out at eight degrees. That is not the only reason the crowd seems to part when he walks through, though it is the primary one: the Javits Center exhibition hall is filled with thousands of motorcyclists, and not one of them has ridden here, except this one. There is also the fact of his *presence*, a grand, almost otherworldly bearing; his movie-star good looks, ice-blue eyes, and dark hair gone gray at the temples (*I am a variety of experience; I am what I have lived through*); and, oh yeah, the tall and beautiful woman with him, long blonde hair swinging at her waist as she follows excitedly a few steps behind. She is here to be inaugurated into ridership, and she is here to make the overwhelmingly male customer base freeze and pretend with near-desperation not to be rendered witless by what clearly belongs to another man.

He finds you, although you have met only once, and that was four years earlier, in some other life, at a rally when you were barely paying attention. That was in part because you did not know who he was. And also because he had not yet fully become what some small, potent seed in him had long ago foreordained he would be: a rider of singular talent and drive, one of the top long-distance endurance riders in the world. He would soon shatter the record on a frightful, 5,645-mile journey on some of the most difficult roadways in North America, and he would do it so fast (a blistering 86.5 hours, ten fewer than his predecessor) that no one could name the person who could have kept him in even distant sight ahead. When he finishes this ride, the first thing he does will be to conceive of something harder to do next.

There are other people like him, who live to ride the ever-more-challenging ride. But few of them think they might like to become the first person to ride upwards of two hundred thousand miles in a year; few of them are as truly strange as to think they could sit in the saddle for *an average of 550 miles every day of the year, Christmas and New Year's not excepted.* John Ryan is thus alone—far and away alone—at the head of a small group, the rabid mile-eaters, that is hidden in plain sight near the very heart of motorcycling.

Alone. How central this will reveal itself to be, in every aspect of the truly odd enterprise that is long-distance endurance motorcycling, and in John Ryan's even more extreme drive to surmount the achievements of all others. ("I simply persist, because it is the best use of my time here on the planet.") It pervades, motivates, defines, makes possible, and curses the rider who has stripped away all else from life in order to do only this. Alone. It is a complicated thing, aloneness. It gave rise to a damnably labyrinthine branch of philosophy, expressed in a few French novels that could only be read during college, when the system both craves and can metabolize extreme depression. Alone. It is what the man walking toward you telegraphs from the moment you take him in. It is all there at once. It will be the beginning and end of the rider's story, as it is in the grander story that enfolds him, the one we all enter and leave alone.

The bike parked in the frozen air outside the Javits Center is, by the owner's own reckoning, a hideous machine. If Ryan himself looks like something not entirely bound by earth's gravity, then this is the UFO that brought him here: a Yamaha FJR1300 so altered by forces both intentional and undesired that it stops passersby in their progress as surely as did the stately blonde. And for similar reasons. The hard functionality of the modifications—HID lights as big as butter plates, bar ends encased in huge mittens to keep hands working in dire cold, black antenna to catch whatever CB chatter is most meaningful to a motorcyclist trying to make time on the slab—stand for the sort of physical pleasure only the most intense activity will yield. The cracks and the long gray scar driven into the blue plastic of the left fairing stand for the dark partner of such deep joys: in this case, a low-side crash seven months earlier, entering a 40 mph turn at twice that, on Alaska's graveled Dalton Highway. It is always surprising how quickly—somewhat like a fourth-grade teacher—the road can smack you for not paying attention. He was looking at his GPS, to make time. Eat miles and make time.

It is the thing on the gas tank, though, that makes those gathered around squint in perplexity. What *is* that thing, anyway? And then some wise guy offers: "That's not *on* the gas tank, that *is* the gas tank," and the murmuring begins again. No one's ever seen anything like it, so no one can imagine what such a thing is for. Even when they do realize that this . . . this *homunculus* that ends just under the rider's chin (the karmic reincarnation of the hood of a wrecked Monte Carlo now colored the nubby black of spray-on truck-bed liner), with a tank bag on top of that, is a thirteen-gallon repository of fuel, they can't imagine who could possibly need a five-hundred-mile range. That's because they don't know this man, an extremist among the self-selected extremists who make up the long-distance endurance elite.

In the all-you-can-eat Chinese buffet that is motorcycling, there are dishes to please everybody; find one that you like—say, the Mongolian stir-fry or the sweet-and-sour shrimp or the lo mein—and you return to fill your plate again and again. Off-road; adventure touring; Sunday cruising; canyon racing. All of these are understood, if not preeminently loved, by most riders. But ride sixteen hundred miles before sleep? Visit the four corners of the country with nary a sit-down meal in almost five days? Why, *that's* not riding. That's some sort of unhinged behavior—going places not to see them but to go to them to say you did.

To say you did, at most; but oftentimes these people keep the information about their little jaunts pretty much to themselves. *(Their little jaunts . . . their little "Ride to Eat" trips from San Diego, California, to Bangor, Maine. In a couple of days, including much of one night. To have dinner and turn around.)* For one thing, it's nobody's business. For another, it's impossible to explain. And it's a free country. No one has to explain anything to an already disapproving audience, unless it's a judge and the DA and you've done a very bad thing.

These rides hurt no one—not even the rider, much, although most people assume they do. (One observer at a long-distance gathering summed it up, "It's healthy, in an unhealthy way.") Contrary to most difficult challenges undertaken in our society, success at long-distance motorcycling carries no prize: no money, no fame, no nothing. Yet it is done.

The rewards must be internal, then, or kept to the knowing accolades of the silent brethren, those who have done these things and therefore know exactly what they cost. As for the rest—don't ask, don't tell.

Don't tell anyone that someone has actually ridden *thirty-one consecutive thousand-mile days.* Keep it to the kind of person who has himself felt the warmth of a private satisfaction upon finishing the demented program of riding harder and longer than anyone else outside of a tenth of a percent of all motorcyclists. Such a person would necessarily be a member of the Iron Butt Association (IBA), fifty thousand of the "World's Toughest Motorcycle Riders" who form a closed circle in part because no one else understands. They care, too, but they acknowledge that it is the nature of these rides that no one could possibly care more than the person who does it. They do it pretty much for themselves. The promise of a hot shower only goes so far. The computer-generated paper certificate and the plastic license-plate back that are the sole tangible rewards do not repay what is expended. Nothing explains the drive that animates the endeavor. To the outsider, that is. And we are all outsiders, unless we are among this elect. Or the infected. Then we will need no explanation, and can offer none to anyone. Inside, and out. There are only these two possibilities.

Forty-eight contiguous states (throw in Alaska for good measure) in fewer than ten days; Europe from north to south in seventy-two hours, 5,300 kilometers; circumnavigate Finland, 3,219 kilometers, in two days; cross the Mexican, United States, and Canadian borders in under twenty-four hours in what is called a Border-to-Border Insanity; ride around the Great Lakes in under fifty hours. Apparently there is only one reason for the existence of maps to the Iron Butt rider: to draw the most perverse lines all over them. (The Iron Butt Association sanctions a National Parks Tour, consisting of visits to fifty national parks in at least twenty-five different states within a year; proof comes with the government-issued stamps in its parks passport. At first this seems to be an uncharacteristic stop-and-smell-the-roses gambit offered by the association, until you realize that of course some riders are turning it into drive-by, stamp-getting quickies. With their training, they no doubt do it in four minutes without taking off their helmets. One fellow on the LDRider listserv who was doing the tour mused to his compatriots that he "realized there's probably no other group of people who wouldn't think it strange that I passed through Dayton, Ohio, on my way back to Virginia from South Carolina." Whereupon another rider rejoined, "That's called a 'Motorcycle Shortcut.'") Finally, one must suspect a sickness, an addiction, pain loved so hard it becomes misshapen into pleasure.

Look at them. You see nothing out of line. They are cops, and doctors, and software engineers. Women and men. Young and old; gray hair and paunches are fairly well represented. Family men and loners. Retirees, lots of them, as they have the time and cash to devote to the hobby of spending time and cash. For that is what it takes. That, and inhuman determination.

Let us stop here. We have to—there is something tangled around our feet, preventing forward progress. You can't parse this straight, from beginning to end, because that is not how it goes. Instead, you reach one conclusion: *Riding feels good, riding more feels even better.* But suddenly your wheel is up against a concrete Jersey barrier and is starting to turn the other way: *Something must be smoldering underneath, ready to burst into flame, to make anyone go that far, that fast, that continuously.*

It is generally accepted as comprehensible, the Once-in-a-Lifetime Adventure beloved of vicarious travelers, to spend three years going around the world with your girlfriend and a soon-to-be-battered–looking motorcycle. The public adores it, the idea of someone doing what they would do, if only they could take the time, get free from work, family, all the bonds we spend years tying about our own ankles. So the far-traveled collect sponsorships (cold-weather underwear, aluminum hard cases), stop by the wayside to write accounts for the blog the world is booting up to read, and publish a book when they return. There's a lot of riding, but there's a lot of people-ing, too (the readability factor demands Interesting Encounters). Hotels, hot meals, nights in tents as opposed to the saddle. Seventy or eighty years ago, an individual could easily make a "first": first man around the world, first woman, first sidecar. Now you have to work hard even to think up some minor fillip that would make it new. In the case of Norwegians Tormod Amlien and Klaus Ulvestad, outlandish humor alone could have been their contribution to the seventy-thousand-mile journey (self-titled the King Croesus Contempt for Death "world's dumbest motorcycle trip," begun in 2009), but they decided to gild the lily by undertaking it on two 1939 Nimbus machines with sidecars "piloted by pure idiots." Extraordinary, even grueling, though it remains, the round-the-world trip is . . . travel. And travel is the antithesis of the Iron Butt enterprise. Around-the-world the Iron Butt way is covering 19,030 miles in thirty-one days and twenty hours, as Nick Sanders did, to enter the Guinness World Records.

This yearning to break a record (largest chocolate-chip cookie ever baked; longest solo flight) is a purely human deviation from animal nature. Yet it has become profoundly in our nature to do such essentially unnatural things as expend energy in otherwise-fruitless acts. The patently absurd things we do—swim across the Atlantic, compete in the Self-Transcendence Race (ha! exactly!) by running 5,649 half-mile laps in fifty-one days, kill ourselves on icy mountaintops for the sole purpose of trying to get there—are a compulsion left by our evolution. We were built to contend with threats that swept down from trees, food that ran swiftly away, blood that spilled and could not be stopped. Pushing an overflowing cart through Wal-

Mart does not count. And so it is that long-distance riding can be seen as a proxy for the daily life-or-death struggle we were kitted out for as forest-dwelling hunters. In its absence, we feel a need to find pursuits that exercise the same mental and physical capacities. Or else they start to itch. We want to feel fully alive, and fully ourselves. In this way, riding to extremes takes humans home again.

The incomprehensibly extraordinary endeavor is nowhere better captured than in G. K. Chesterton's phrase *the immense act*. Its undertaking is "human and excusable" due to the fact that "the thing was perfectly useless to everybody, including the person who did it." (Therefore they are literally pointless, these things that drive determinedly toward *one point and no other*, which is another way of describing what it is to be on the road on a bike.) The mountaineer Wilfrid Noyce's 1958 study of immense acts, *The Springs of Adventure*, identifies the end of the eighteenth and the beginning of the nineteenth century as "the time when the idea of adventure 'for its own sake' crystallized in the minds of men." It is no coincidence that this was precisely the period when the Industrial Revolution was creating a new world for us in which our skills as survivalists of the plains and forests would go by the wayside. Wal-Mart Supercenter, here we come.

Long-distance riding, we need you.

. . .

**JOHN RYAN WAS** a normal motorcyclist when he began, thirty years ago. Normal, in that he learned early on that riding gave him things that nothing else could. When you find something that does that, you are well on the road to perdition, or at least to riding an awful lot. Ticking off the miles becomes a satisfaction in itself, the only calculable accounting of an incalculable experience. It is one that encompasses physiology, chemistry, sociology, and religion. Almost everything else as well, up to and possibly including astrology.

Or so this motorcyclist began to learn, the day he got his license; it was not, however, the day he started riding. That had happened a couple of thousand miles earlier, when his 1971 Honda CB350 started taking him all over the New Jersey–New York metro area.

Ryan is now rare among motorcyclists in many things, not least his ability to write about the subject with a clarity and voice last heard among essayists of the 1930s: collegiate, wryly incisive, slightly formal, and always correct. In his all-too-aptly titled blog, "There's Absolutely No Excuse for the Way I'm About to Act," he recounted one memorable passage in his sentimental education:

> *I approached a corner at a speed well above my modest skills, ran wide, and slid on the gravel at the edge, slamming into the outside curb.*
>
> *My poor bike! How could I do such a stupid thing to my best friend?*

The broken hand was treated as an afterthought, or perhaps just deserts; it was the first of twenty-eight fractures sustained thus far (this is a man who goes into things way more thoroughly than most). His first response was to figure a means to operate the clutch lever while he was in a cast up to his elbow and could no longer squeeze his fingers. He approached this as a mechanical problem, befitting his aborted college career as an engineer. As an application of pure will to the wish to continue, it is reminiscent of the quotidian life of the test pilot (the sound barrier was broken by a fighter jock, name of Chuck Yeager, with his busted ribs held by tape) or the road racer (as an amateur, Ryan proved he was almost up to doing pro-level work by riding a sportbike some sixty-five miles in half an hour—in the days of youth "when I was still invincible"—in the lucky company of friends who were off-duty police). On he rode.

*Winter approached, and my fellow motorcyclists disappeared from the road. I wondered how they managed without riding for nearly half the year; it must be like going without a drink or without booting up some junk for the entire winter. What is wrong with these people?*

What is wrong, of course, is that they are not John Ryan, looking for a secret satisfaction at the far edges of experience, the kind that most are quite happy to do without. He did a thousand-mile day all in single-digit temperatures; ah, but that was required, as he had to get to Virginia "to settle a disagreement with a state trooper." It was presumably not as necessary to go to Vermont when it was ten below zero. But now Ryan knows that he can.

Very soon, there was nothing in the world he wanted to do but ride a bike. He had tried, and succeeded well enough at, other occupations: college basketball player, painting contractor, nightclub bouncer. One of his relatively few unsuccessful jobs was with the U.S. Postal Service, which sacked him as a night shift mail sorter. The problem was hardly the hours; his later career as an endurance rider proved that the ability to go without sleep was something he could master completely. Instead, the cause was garden-variety "personality conflict" with a superior—one suspects an inherent inability to kowtow to bureaucracy—which later revealed itself as a great personal favor. Nonetheless, it was a disappointment to his father, who had been dean of discipline and basketball coach at a public high school in New Jersey. We do not escape our upbringings any more than wet clay escapes the thumb's impress, and here the Jesuitical precepts, spelled out in the *Spiritual Exercises* of St. Ignatius, speak directly to the motorcyclist who perseveres long after any other would have taken shelter from the sleet or the empty night: one should seek to "conquer oneself and to regulate one's life in such a way that no decision is made under the influence of any inordinate attachment." Such as to the relief of discomfort.

Ryan *père* would have liked to have seen his son (one of six children) become a doctor. But if that employment bar was too high, it also had a minimum setting: any job that would provide a pension and health insurance on retirement, as his did. After all, this is one of the articles of American religion: Give your best years, your *now*, so that at some distant point, which may never in fact arrive, you can get all the pills you'll need to extend your shuffle to the grave. In eschewing this approach, Ryan showed himself an unlikely Buddhist, throwing in his lot with present happiness. Maybe that is because somewhere deep in the place in each of us where we store inchoate truths, he found the possibility that this future may never arrive for him. He is a type 1 diabetic. Either he rides hard and far now so that he'll be a ways down the road when the axe falls, or he rides always harder and farther not to escape it but to make it fall on his schedule. Or more likely both. We are obstinate, perverse creatures. None is more obstinate than the person who decides to devote his life to a particular madness. It is healthy, in an unhealthy way.

What he calls his riding "habit" started with about ten thousand miles a year, but it quickly tripled, and then higher math got hold of it. He got an FZR1000, and then another, riding these two Yamahas for 339,000 miles, a figure that he believes might represent the most ever done on open-class sportbikes. One day this clicks into perspective when I realize that my family car, at the end of four years of use as my only transportation, had just ticked over sixty-one thousand miles. The average motorcyclist in the United States rides three thousand miles a year. He put another twenty thousand miles on a Yamaha FJ1100.

Sometimes the trajectory of the life you were meant to lead begins in a series of small accidents, shifts so small you don't recognize how large they are until later. In Ryan's case, it was obtaining a BMW K75, from his uncle's estate, in 2002. Then he started "hanging out with a bad crowd," the serious (and seriously clubbish) riders of machinery that was built to grind out the miles. One of the proudest achievements of the card-carrying BMW rider is official recognition for notching a mileage benchmark: a hundred thousand miles, a million miles. More than a few have gotten there; more than a few are now gripped with the desire to do so. Perhaps this is why you are most apt to be congratulated upon first buying a Beemer with the words, "Welcome to the dark side."

At the gatherings of the New Jersey Shore BMW Riders that he attended, Ryan started noticing some intriguing merit badges displayed on certain riders' bikes. These are the riders who attract attention mainly because they ask for none. They stand apart, unconscious of the most striking thing about them, immediately grasped by the watcher: they are masters. They own the world. When they ride, they stand at the apex where physics, mechanics, and geography meet; they display insouciant control. They do difficult things with consummate ease, the machines beneath them moving at their will alone, with absolute—balletic—grace. We have only one small word for the large thing they are: *cool.* They don't speak of it, but their bikes do. These look well loved, by virtue of being well used. And they bear signs—sheepskin-covered saddles, auxiliary lights, no-nonsense aluminum panniers—that their owners are not fooling around. They ride. And many belong, as one can discern by a single discreet display, to what must surely be the coolest club of all: the Iron Butt Association. Their license-plate backs are the only sign that among motorcyclists they stand proudly apart. *SaddleSore 1000. Bun Burner 1500.* And, for the truly elite, *Iron Butt Rally: 11 Days, 11,000 Miles.* If you are not intrigued, then you have not been hearing the sirens singing their soft, beckoning song: "Miles, miles, more miles. . . ."

What happened next in Ryan's life seems intentional, or necessary, though it was neither. He took the first step—into what, he had no way of knowing. That is how it goes.

For almost all who receive a membership number from the Iron Butt Association—after submission of paperwork comprising witness signatures at the beginning and end of the ride, dated gas receipts, map, log of stops, and a check for fifty dollars or thereabouts—the initiation ride is a SaddleSore, the completion of a thousand miles within twenty-four hours. It is a tough ride. But Ryan has a native dislike for stopping. So for his first documented ride, he continued on, not to the next step (a Bun Burner, fifteen hundred miles within thirty-six hours) but right to the third: a Bun Burner Gold, fifteen hundred miles within twenty-four hours. Actually, he did better than that: sixteen hundred miles, with an hour and a half to spare.

What is easy for him is hard for others. Though there's no way to really know, is there, and it could well be that what is hard for him he simply pretends is easy. He's not going to talk about it much. He's just going to stand there quietly in that dirt-impregnated suit. He always looks as if he's just ducked his head to deflect a blow, or to avoid a flurry of questions, or to invite a flurry of questions. What he doesn't want is what he courts (death, lots of attention). He is admittedly shy, and he wants nothing more than to be with others. He stays, everywhere, to the bitter end. He provokes nothing so much as the question, Why does he do this stuff? And the question, Why? is what he runs both from and toward. Yes, fast.

In order to do this, to be unlike anyone else in the world, he has cleared the decks of all the ropes and anchors the rest of humanity laboriously collects in order to feel safe, or in order to trip over. By his own account, he has "no career, savings, or health insurance, because I have chosen to ride instead of responsibly chasing my tail like everyone else." He does not have a car, or a house, or a wife, or children. What he does have, as of the end of that first Bun Burner Gold, is a calling. The allusion to sacred ordination is more than apt; Ryan often refers to a special class, that of *devout* motorcyclist. Echoing the pithy bike sticker that reads "Being a biker is not a matter of life and death, it's more important than that," to a friend who called him "born again" when he got back on two wheels after an unprecedented, and painful, four months without a bike, he replied, "I don't care for anything described as 'born again.' That sounds too religious, and motorcycling is much more important than that."

Ryan is a contrarian, to his friends perhaps more than to his enemies, though there are few of the latter due to his much-remarked-upon humility. (This gets big play when he brushes off the amazed adulation of other riders after completing an especially brutal ride, usually by saying the success belonged to those who helped, or, failing that, to the bike itself.) But if one listens closely, one hears almost everything dismissed, as long as it has been said by others. It is just that it is done with such compact wittiness—Ryan is a man of few words, and those always meticulously chosen—it is hard to take offense. Even when one should.

The generous, and probably correct, view of the paradoxical velvet sharpness in his character is that he could not do the godawful rides he does without being thoroughgoingly contrary. That is in the job description.

> Engravers use diamonds to inscribe the hardest substances on the planet. One day I'm going to use John Ryan's head to inscribe a diamond. He is the prototypical embodiment of the expression "My way or the highway," except that his way actually is the highway and it doesn't matter one microgram of logic to him what you or eight highways departments know about that road, its weather, its condition, or its history. He has done, as they say on Wall Street, his due diligence. His research tells him it's time to go. He goes. Your job at that point is to shut up and get out of his way.

That is the opinion of Bob Higdon, and on the subject of these anchorites of motorcycledom, there is no one better to listen to. He is a retired Washington, DC, trial attorney and the poet laureate of the Iron Butt Association. He is unique to the organization because he is both insider—a ferocious rider who partakes of the madness, having amassed 1.1 million miles on BMWs since 1972, once putting in a hundred-thousand-mile year, and riding around the world in eighty days (he prefers a literary angle for his journeys)—and outsider. That is what being a writer makes you: the heavy thinking pushes you just across the border, toward a vantage that takes in the whole country. He can comment, acerbically, on what these peculiar outsiders are doing, even though he is one of them. And like any consummate critic, he knows his artists as well as his genres. He cannot help but look on helplessly as John Ryan persists in rewriting the rules for the rule-breakers—or, as Higdon nailed it: "John Ryan is an unusual person in a game where three standard deviations from the norm is the norm." Higdon calls the brethren of extreme long-distance motorcyclists "the last cowboys."* Given Higdon's bemused admiration for, not to mention frequent legal advice to, Ryan, he is known as the younger man's illegitimate father.

. . .

**AFTER A SADDLESORE,** either you go on or you don't. Either that was the hardest day of your life or it was one of the most indescribable. Or it was one because it was also the other, and so you continue. Ryan found it an agreeable challenge to next ride across the country in under fifty hours. Four months later, he thought it interesting to improve, or debauch, this 50cc Quest by doing it again, adding hundreds of miles to the route. The year 2004 turned out to be a big one. In addition to those coast-to-coast ambles, he hammered a Bun Burner Gold 3000—back-to-back fifteen-hundred-mile days, or three thousand miles in under forty-eight hours—and then a Bun Burner Gold Trifecta, the forty-five hundred miles between New Jersey and Winslow, Arizona, and back in three days. He wrote the original book on that little achievement; since then, eight other riders have followed his lead. Now it seemed to function as a compulsion: the bike in one direction, throttle on. And on. If you are wired a certain way—some are, though many aren't—you find it hypnotic

---

* He is, of course, correct. This, from the 1897 book *The Story of the Cowboy,* by Emerson Hough, is only a slightly more hyperbolic description of today's long-distance rider: "The most successful of these [broncobusters], who came of the hardiest and most daring of the range riders, rarely lasted more than a few years in the business. Sometimes their lungs were torn loose by the violent jolting of the . . . wild beasts they rode, and many busters would spit blood after a few months at their calling. . . . A broken leg or arm was a light calamity, accepted philosophically with the feeling that it might have been much worse . . . those who engage in this business go about it methodically and steadily, probably with no thought that they are doing anything extraordinary, because they have never done anything else."

to keep the wheels turning, a disturbing annoyance to stop. And so you stop less, and less. At some point, you hit the wall, and then it opens like a door, into the zone. In the zone, there are vast spaces of insuperable calm.

That is what Ryan likely found on his rolling meditations, as nowhere else: transcendent peace. He was alone, and one, with it. Ultimately, that is what the long-distance rider realizes: I like to ride alone. I can only ride alone. The long ride is life; the longer ride is life eternal.

In 2004, he finally knew where he wanted to be: alone, and riding there. So he also did a National Parks Tour Silver, visiting sixty-one parks in twenty-seven states, including the four describing the corners of the lower 48: Maine, Florida, California, Washington. He would not assign a high-flown motive to the behavior, even if it was beginning to feel like a philosophical as well as a physical necessity. Instead, he again played it contrariwise. "I am here to burn gasoline, and I only have another fifty years or so to do it. Global warming and depletion of the ozone layer will not be severe enough for me to worry about, and we must see to it that the ensuing generations have plenty to think about, and problems to solve."

Extreme long-distance riding as a public service. Brilliant.

More sinister, these are also his words: "I use a motorcycle as a weapon to get things done." Although Ryan rarely plays anything straight, self-satire being a dominant mode of delivery, there is nonetheless a genuine undercurrent of violence in his choice of term; there is vengeance. Weapons are meant to hurt, or worse. Like kill the record of anyone before him who has implicitly claimed, I have gone as far as fast as it is possible.

Not so, says Ryan. *Watch me.*

# 2. Ingesting road

*Only those who risk going too far can possibly find out how far they can go.*

—GEORGE ELIOT

*"Let us leave good sense behind like a hideous husk and let us hurl ourselves, like fruit spiced with pride, into the immense mouth and breast of the world! Let us feed the unknown, not from despair, but simply to enrich the unfathomable reservoirs of the Absurd!"*

—F. T. MARINETTI, "THE FUTURIST MANIFESTO," 1909

**I SPECIALIZE IN PLANS** that sound much better the farther away they are from implementation. The good sense drains from them with each turn of the calendar page, however, and the week before their occurrence they are revealed in all their head-slapping idiocy: *What was I thinking?* But by then the machinery of logistics has been cranking and wheezing for too long. Mine is a particularly large apparatus: dogsitters and child care and multiple schedule rejiggerings. Thus, I spent the day of August 20, 2009, deep in the embrace of regret.

For several months I had steeped myself in a lukewarm broth simmered from "Could I?" and "Life is short." Could I ride a long distance, not to go anywhere in particular but to ride a long distance? Could I discover that I was made of material tough and elastic, up to a challenge that was for once physical, not an emotional obstacle course of my own difficult making? Well, we would see, wouldn't we. I blithely decided that I would try to ride a SaddleSore. Why not?

I had surprised myself earlier in the summer by riding the 750 miles from the site of the BMWMOA international rally in Tennessee to upstate New York in one shot, by far the longest day I'd ever spent in the saddle. In part it was due to the fact that I was astride a K75, the aptly nicknamed "Flying Brick." It is a bike that in its soul says, *Go, just* go. Solid at speed, whirring in near-silence (its fuel pump the loudest bit on the whole bike), it expresses the underlying sense that if eternity could be spent riding, then eternity is how long it would keep a steady 75 without complaint.

When I pulled in to my driveway at nine that night, I thought to myself, *Hey, that wasn't so hard.* The other reason I had held down the throttle for twelve hours on the highway while state borders slid up my windscreen then flew past like slips of paper was that I had to. I needed to be home that night. Need, whether imposed by domestic agenda or by strictly internal drives, is what keeps the rider going. Everything you do can feel like a need if repeated to yourself enough.

That is why, at eight o'clock on a late summer night, water and ground beans had been poured into the coffee machine so it was now poised for a flip of the switch. Two peanut-butter-and-jelly sandwiches and a bag of trail mix were in a sack hanging on the front door's knob. The K75 stood parked outside the garage door and covered, to save the five minutes it takes to open the door, pull it out, and close the door behind. Its bags were packed; in its topcase stood a miniature army of bottled water so no seconds would be lost walking inside the gas station to look for a fountain or standing in hypnotized indecision before three refrigerator cases of different gaily colored liquids. On the eve of trying this thing that had seemed so heroic when first thought of, I find a sadness descending on me.

All day long I had felt the press of a heavy nostalgia, memories from other rides in other times, so full of real sensation—the scent of fir in the air, that moment of pulling to a stop at a wayside rest area, raising my leg over the seat in order to stop and stare up into a popsicle-blue sky and talk while the bikes wait, patient as horses— that it catches me in the chest. *That is traveling,* I think; *that is what I want to do, be with another, ride slow, then fast, then slow; lie in the grass a while, decide to stop because a sign said there was something enticing to stop for*

The sadness arose because, against my will and expectations, in a matter of days two summers before, my life had become a new thing (*alone again*), and motorcycling was about to become a new thing as well, detached from its former self as something shared (*alone now*). This long-distance ride seemed the essence of aloneness, insular and packed inside its own ergonomic box, sealed so perfectly against seepage from the outside world.

I wanted seepage—or at least chaos, desire, hope, fear, allure, serendipity, weakness, the whole gooey mess the weird world of human relationship always slopped in one's path. Clocks, speedos, calculations, a job well done: what does this have to do with living? And living, it seemed to me, had everything to do with riding.

Then the alarm rang at 4:30 a.m. Sadness winked out with the last stars. Gloom is, anyway, a leisure-time activity. Suddenly it was a new moment, and it made the world new, too. There was only a motorcycle, a key, my hand. With a turn, a small movement would start a larger one, and all else would melt away. It was time to go.

Also (I neglected to mention), another bike had been parked next to mine: an FJR1300.

John Ryan watched, his expression impassive, as I poured myself a mug of coffee. After all, he had seen others drink it before, but he himself never touched caffeine in any form (which prompts disbelief in some online commenters who cannot conceive that anyone could ride, hard, for four days on a total of less than eight hours' sleep without the liberal use of stimulants). Nor does he ingest its opposite number, alcohol; his body is thus spared the daily swing from stimulant to soporific and back again that so many of us require of our constitutions. He has other demands to place on his.

His demeanor this day was to be one long No Comment; he was here to watch over my first documented thousand-mile day and to let me make my own mistakes. Quite as many as I wanted, in fact.

The sun was just beginning to shade the sky dove gray as we pulled down our helmets. This was a ride conceived in strangeness—go due west, to Erie, Pennsylvania, in order to end due south, in Spartanburg, South Carolina—but I held on to vestigial memories of riding as being about encounters with scenery, which is why I felt a childish anticipation, not shared with my stern mentor, of that first hour. It was a favorite route, taken periodically during a couple of my many previous lifetimes, therefore I would ride through the past, slicing into it with present desire. But first there was business to conduct: attaining the first gas receipt, which, along with the witness form signed by Ryan (akin to having Stephen Hawking oversee your fifth-grade science-fair project), was all the proof I would have that I was in fact doing what I was doing. There was a Mobil station half a mile from the house, but it would not open until 5:30 a.m., by which point I hoped to be forty miles down the road. Then again, a credit card opens all doors, or at least most pumps. Later it occurred to me that it's the credit card that is responsible for long-distance riding as practiced in the modern era: it alone makes possible the four-minute fuel stop, with the bike balanced between your legs, card inserted, tank filled, closed, receipt pulled, and engine fired back up without the sidestand touching earth. It also provides the time- and place-stamped slip required by documentation guidelines, or, failing that, the option of using plastic for the desperate purchase of a pack of gum or several postcards in order to acquire something more valuable: proof, in form acceptable to the IBA, that you'd been somewhere.

In addition to acting as portable witness, Ryan also quietly demonstrated how to economically accomplish the record-keeping business he had previously explained as central to the long-distance enterprise: it kept the rider focused on the job, and focus was the bedrock of safety. I saved precious minutes and dropped pens by not having to fumble with a notebook in order to create a log; instead, he had instructed me to number the receipts in order on the back of each one, along with the odometer reading. I would write up a log after I returned home. But I was to keep the receipts safe; lost receipts were a heartbreak, and heartbreaks happen.

Take a right, and it begins. All is hope at the beginning of a ride. The heart soars; the speed increases. We were alone on the road, the mountains of the deep Catskills a green wall in the distance ahead, saying, Come on. His auxiliary lights shone like yellow-white suns in my mirrors from a quarter of a mile back. He had dropped his speed for some reason, and I puzzled as I went.

Either he needed to give himself a cushion into which he could throw himself later at his desired speed, which I assumed was considerably greater than my already borderline-uncomfortable one, or something else was going on. Only much later did I realize that he did not want to influence my speed in either direction. This was my ride. Only much later did I realize I'd screwed up my ride. For some reason, I'd gotten it into my head that I needed to go as fast as I possibly could.

Which is why, six hours later (third gas stop), I was lying facedown in the grass and begging him to press as hard as he could on my spine, so it would issue cracking sounds and relieve the unrelenting pressure that was causing my back muscles to spasm. I thought I deserved a twenty-minute break; he thought I was an incredible fool, wasting time this way at a stop. I was creating a vicious cycle, where uncalled-for speed hyped my senses, requiring periodic relief. I did spinal twists; I did deep knee bends. Then, after throwing away that time, I got back on the bike and cranked it up for the next two hours, repeating the process. Not to mention that my speed increased my gas usage, requiring more frequent stops. At a sensible rate, I could get 175 miles from a tank, but now I would wring only 150 before the idiot light went on and it was time to exit in search of more fuel.

When we were just over the Virginia state line, he mentioned that due to a few unfortunate encounters with law-enforcement officers in the state—radar detectors being illegal there and traffic enforcement "greedily strict," as Ryan had learned through hard experience—he would keep his progress to no more than five miles above the limit. He would catch up with me when we crossed into West Virginia.

Of that I had no fear. It was possible to ride as fast as you've ever ridden on the open highway, only to see John Ryan, just ahead and frustrated with the pace of traffic, suddenly lay his bike on its side and cross three lanes before you could adjust to the sight. In another second, he would be a small dot disappearing toward the horizon. He could insert himself in the three-inch gap between a truck and a car overtaking it. It was a physical impossibility, but there he went. No city at rush hour could make him pause, no phalanx of cars could deter his forward press.

His defense, and as usual it bore truth, solid and unimpeachable, was that it was safer to ride faster than the prevailing rate, as it concentrated the dangers in front, rather than to the sides and rear. Plus, it was great fun to thread the needle. It gave the mind something to do, calculating clearances and variable speeds. It gave the body much pleasure, flicking the heavy machine that suddenly seemed diaphanously responsive to one's very thoughts.

At what point did I lose track of where I was? There was only what was ahead: more of what was behind. And behind had already been forgotten; behind had nothing to do with anything anymore. At what point did I think I could not go on but knew I would? Two forces were pulling me on: saving face—I had said I was going to do a thousand-in-one, so I had to do it—and the road itself. Going on had quickly become a habit, like nicotine. I was ingesting road, and it made me want only more road.

The gift inside the multiple layers of disagreeable wrapping (having to shake out the numbed fingers as you go, the cramping knees; realizing that the stock saddle that had previously seemed perfectly fine is in fact not, with a seam that bears into the flesh and ensures truth in advertising for an endeavor called SaddleSore) was the time and space to think. It is something that has little place in a world that has dispensed with the extended menial task. This is what long-distance riders find out on the road, similar to the discovery of those who split four cords of wood by hand: the pleasure of their own company. Tangled skeins of problems unravel themselves with no pulling; barriers fall away, as if in dreams. In those, you are always in one place, then suddenly in another, transformed, flying.

The people, and there are many, who simply don't *get* LD riding are seeing it in a place it does not belong: the standard motorcycling paradigm. "Bikes take us to beautiful places (or adventuresome ones, which in their difficulties are beautiful to a rider) that are experienced through the senses that touch the external world—sight, smell, sensation." But the way you must see this melodic variation on the motorcyclish theme is that the adventure is internal. It aims itself toward the mountainous passes and river crossings of the mental and emotional landscape, as brutal and awe-inspiring and challenging as any route outside. This inner country is rarely explored comprehensively, for the simple reason that the common structure of life has no quarter for it. But engage the peculiar mechanics of deep time on a machine that focuses the mind like a laser at the same time it frees the bonds of the physical, and you go, fast, into infinite slowness. Here is the lovely electrical charge of paradox; motorcycling taps deep into it. I once thought I'd said everything I could think of to say on the subject of bikes. Now I know I never can.

It also occurred to me, possibly on a straightaway of Route 17, the Southern Tier Expressway, passing the Seneca Allegany tribe's casino, that people who LD ride *do* see the scenery; they just do it at greater velocity.

Weather has no hold on riders who are traversing, in a unitary block of time, a readable line across a multistate map. There's no guarantee of going from here to there all in sunshine. So, like Boy Scouts, they are prepared. I refer to mental preparedness predominantly: gear has become in recent years so competent that riders barely feel a torrent or wall of cold. But when the prescribed route, as it must, passes through all the variability of earth's terrain—mountain, desert, forested wilds—the mind knows it will face "situations." And when this is known, a day of solid rain or a coastline with headwinds is just business as usual.

I do not know why it did not rain, then, on a single one of my 1,075 miles. It should have, given the distance, given that I had not yet fully outfitted myself with technologically current gear and was still investing faith in a fifteen-year-old pair of rain covers for my boots; given that I was in denial, and not mentally prepared one whit. When we checked the radar the night before, there had been a green-yellow mass of heavy showers decorating the entire line of my journey, and the sight filled me with a gray dread. I did not know whether I was capable of holding onto a motorcycle for that many hours. Doing so in a continuous downpour seemed even more unlikely.

It is hard for the human mind to conceive of luck, which is as much as saying nothingness; we are endlessly inventive when it comes to causality. Ten thousand years yielding the creation of ten thousand religions, for just one example. I fought, successfully, the half-conscious notion that I had done something kind or generous to make the sun shine, at least between the hours of six and eight-thirty. Alas, that was not likely. Arbitrary luck—now there was a chance. Rain was falling in our environs; ominous clouds hovered over there, and back there. But above us, only the mention. And then, the rainbow.

It arced from one impossible distance to another, and that place lay directly ahead. As I began to think I could go on no longer, after thirteen hours of riding, the rainbow spread itself across my bit of heaven to provide animating thought: *It is here for some purpose; it is here to say, This is right. How right, you did not know. But* this *right.*

Here is how a day passes.

Little bits fly up from the side of the road, glimpsed, and then suddenly they're in your head, weaving thoughts. "Why Delilah" is inexplicably graffitied on a rock, and you find yourself thinking about that radio show ("It's time to relax and unwind. It's time to love someone," whispers a woman of sultry voice named only Delilah, beamed out from 222 radio stations but really to you alone) you would be embarrassed to admit you have listened to in the car, alone at night on some long trip, because her voice is so soothing, so embracing, and she wants to help those poor people who call her from the blackness of out there, unknown and unseen but caught tightly by some awful pain they can't shake loose, and at once you feel yourself just like them and horrified at your own great relief that you have never, ever experienced anything quite that messed up. And in this way, a sight starts a riff, like two notes of music that remind you of some song, which plays for a while until it becomes another, and suddenly you're remembering music you'd forgotten you knew. That is how you come to be fifty miles farther down the road, with miles and music suddenly one single thing, an acoustic sculpture, standing out there, carved of time and space. This is nice, until a little later, when it's grown dark, and you're blinking your eyes quickly to stop them from feeling so tired, so much like they want to close, and then you realize you've just seen something that is not there. That's quite a moment.

Still, you go on. Because one thing about getting tired is that you lose the ability to know you're tired. You know only that you haven't gotten where you wanted to get.

A highway work-zone sign flashes its LED message and I'm already past it when my mind reads it out loud for the benefit of its low-IQ audience: Impossible Delays.

Wait. Shake the head to clear it. That didn't help; again. Blink.

There. Sort of. It's normal, isn't it, when you want so badly to be at your goal—seventy miles now, though the exits are getting confusing all of a sudden, and it's cruel that there's heavy urban traffic at this late point, coming on 10 p.m., the end of the ride dammit, and they're all trying to get somewhere quickly too, so they're riding on your tail just when you need some breathing space, some room to wonder—that you should misread a sign in exactly the way it ought to have been written.

It's too late to stop. You are going to finish this thing. (The other rider is closer behind now, his lights both companionable and a goad.) And that is when the miles start dropping away, by tens. You try to keep calculating, as the parade of numbers—miles into gallons, number of fuel stops into total mileage—is what has propelled you all along, but now the keys are sticking a little, and you press "plus" when you meant "divide," and have to clear and start again, and then you see it: the glowing red letters ahead. *Marriott.*

It's where your bike wanted to be, magnetically drawn to this quiet waiting lineup of machines; it wants to sleep now, among its own kind. When you finally dismount, your body still holds movement inside, and it's vibrating a little. It feels strange to walk. But you do, into the marble halls. You're looking for them, the hundred people who in another day will be mounting these motorcycles to begin the mother of all long-distance rides, the Iron Butt Rally. That is why you came to Spartanburg, South Carolina: to see if you could do what you just did, and to look at them, the strange variety of person who will soon be doing what you know you never could.

• • •

JOHN RYAN WALKS IN beside me, without speaking. When we enter the bar of the Marriott, at 10:50 p.m., people raise their hands or their glasses in greeting. He scans the group, looking for appropri-ate people to sign my *Eyewitness Form for End of Ride*. The first candidate he spies is the communications officer of the Iron Butt Association, Ira Agins. "Melissa has just completed her first Saddle-Sore," he tells Agins with a small smile. The genuine enthusiasm in the congratulations I am offered takes me aback; why, this is noth-ing to people like Agins. But what he gives, in his handshake, in the look in his eyes, is for real. It is as if I have done something amazing; or maybe something that he knows will mark me, in the same deep place he was marked so long ago he cannot really remember. My second signature is that of Bob Higdon, who likewise congratulates me, the first and last time I have heard an unironic word issue from his mouth. He too means it. I am stunned.

I am so tired I lack the energy to down a beer. Besides, I still have to get back on the bike tonight, as our hotel, cheaper by thirty dol-lars a night than this one, is a couple of miles away, in some direc-tion. Around me, people are clustered, drinking, talking, talking. Then the crowd starts thinning out; it is getting late. Ryan stands talking, too, head ducked as he listens, until a crooked smile and a short, muffled explosion of laughter lights him, then passes. I am so tired I think it would be perfectly appropriate to curl up and spend the night under a bar stool. I worry that I won't be able to find our hotel. But Ryan is nowhere near ready to go. He is not tired in the least. He is home, in his nation, the long-distance tribe that only nominally lives elsewhere, but actually here: a place to meet and then part again.

Ryan reads the hotel directions to me from his GPS, then returns to the bar while I mount the bike again. I ride down the dark and depopulated street and go on, and on, and now I am heading out of Spartanburg and into the black countryside. My odometer tells me

I have gone five miles, when I should only have gone two. I turn and head back to the Marriott. This time, I ask the receptionist for directions. Ryan had sent me to the left out of the hotel; I should have gone right. He is still in the bar, holding a glass of water.

I pull the sheets up over my body, which feels somewhat odd, as though it is not mine. I reach for the pad of Comfort Inn paper on the bedside table. I had had, as I always do on a long motorcycle ride, some immortal thoughts I needed to get down; they will make my fortune. Once again, though, they are gone. I can retrieve not a single one, which increases their value. Lost things are always the best things you ever had.

I did not know it then, but on this same day, elsewhere, eight others also completed a thousand-mile ride. During the same week, sixty others would do the same, including three in Canada, four in Russia, and one in Ukraine.

The clock by the bed flicks over: 1:42 a.m. I have been awake almost twenty-one hours, most of them on the bike, at a moving average of 69 mph. I am so tired it all falls away as I descend into sleep, moving backward, until the miles are gone.

# 3. This near to hellfire

*These things reanimate; they would reanimate us; but it happens in each patient the particular freak-activity chosen is the only thing that does reanimate; and therein lies the morbid state. . . . There is no doubt that to some men sprees and excesses of almost any kind are medicinal, temporarily at any rate, in spite of what the moralists and doctors say.*

—WILLIAM JAMES, "THE ENERGIES OF MEN," 1906

*We are not here to do what has already been done.*

—ROBERT HENRI

**LISTEN CAREFULLY TO THE WORDS** chosen to describe it: "A risk-laden torture test." "Pure insanity." "A major life event." One man who was picked by lottery to participate in the biennial event was told by a friend, "Let the eighteen-month mind-fuck begin." Another who was not picked said, "I don't know if I'm sad, or relieved." Those who are called know it as "the Big Dance." The words refer to the Iron Butt Rally (*11 Days, 11,000 Miles* appears on the license-plate backs of those who have done it, in an elemental description that in

its arrow-to-the-heart manner will immediately horrify the unini-
tiated or excite the already infected), but this thing is so beyond
words it's all pretty futile. Anyway, the syllables are meant to reflect
inner attitudes, most often mental malady, something you can't
see. But one wants physical evidence. Badly. The whole thing is not
graspable without it. The mental aspect to this unholy endeavor
is shaped by the physical, in the way hot metal is stamped in the
foundry. Seeing it will make it real. I sense this is utterly outside
my native capabilities, or even desire, to stretch them to breaking
to accommodate the attempt. That is perhaps why I feel the need to
go where such a thing is—at least for a relatively minuscule number
of others—possible. To see if the ineffable substance called *spirit* is
somehow visible through helmets and gloves. To see if it might be
found in oneself.

One needs to witness some proof that the undertaking—what
Bob Higdon terms a mission "immune to reason"—is voluntary. Or
that it can happen at all.

The men and women who have, for some odd reason, decided to
participate in the rally will ride an average of a thousand miles a day
for eleven days straight. Though some will ride a bit less, the majority do more. In 2005, one entrant, Mark Kiecker, rode 5,485 miles
in the final *four days*, after being on the road and cranking for six
days, with little sleep, finishing the rally with a total of 13,354 miles,
three short of a new record. They will cross and recross the North
American continent while amassing those miles, from top (Alaska
above the Arctic Circle) to nearly bottom, and from coast to coast,
sometimes past the coast to an island or two, and will experience
every climatic condition the hemisphere has to offer—slamming
wind, fog, sleet, snow, sheeting rain, threat of hurricane, blank desert sun and nighttime chill, sometimes all in the same day. One par-

ticipant wrote of waking up after a nap beside his bike to find that it was thirty-three degrees, and later that day he rode into 115 degrees of Nevada heat, after which, he reported, he realized he "smelled like the chimp house at the zoo." They will ride on into the small hours of the night, knowing clean sheets only periodically and then maybe for only a couple of hours, more often catching sleep at a rest area on the ground behind some bushes or on a picnic table, waggishly known as the Iron Butt Motel. Then they will remount yet again to ride through the dark, with its myriad creeping dangers—outside, in the form of unwitting animals that thought they alone owned the nighttime road, and inside, where exhaustion and, perhaps, despair settle over the mind like a heavy weight. They will eat and drink while riding. They will think, and worry, and calculate. Route. Weather. Miles, fuel, minutes. They will improvise fixes for what inevitably breaks, or sometimes will not be able to, and so will limp toward the finish minus one cylinder, or praying the last cords in the tire won't definitively shred before the final checkpoint. And the reason they get this near to hellfire is . . . bonus points. In other words, ephemera. Bonus points are attached to places, the more difficult to get to, the higher in value. (*Visit Washington, DC—on the way from Spokane to San Diego; go to the farthest northwest point of the lower 48, on a log from Maine to Utah; go to a bar in Gerlach, Nevada, and receive the coordinates for some spot in the middle of the Black Rock Desert, to locate a coin in the dirt; ride for four hundred miles on a snow-slicked gravel road to get a picture of your bike in front of a hotel in Prudhoe Bay, Alaska, then turn right around and head for Alabama; take a ride on a roller coaster strung on top of a hundred-story building; hike up a steep trail in a park in the dark; go to any crazy place they ask, then leave and go to some other demonically devised point on the map hundreds and hundreds of miles away, and if you are thirty seconds late at the next checkpoint, why, it was all for nothing then.*) The points have no monetary value, but the riders will want them more fiercely than anyone ever wanted anything. They are won with a photo of a uniquely numbered towel (also known as the "crying towel"; now you see why) held up in front of whatever themed locale is listed along with the hundreds of possible "bonii" that are in the packet that was distributed at the banquet the night before this week and a half during which no one will shower, no one will sleep a full night, no one will know, for certain, if they have it in them to win—*what? a plaque and a place in a history that is like a single tree in a thousand-acre forest of other histories of men's peculiar exploits*—or even the good luck to finish at all. For that is what, in the end, it comes down to: routing smarts, obdurate will, and the kind of luck that can only fall from the sky.

My search for a glimpse of the undeniable concrete ends at the parking lot of the Marriott Hotel in Spartanburg, South Carolina, on August 21, 2009. There, behind cordons, are arrayed a hundred machines that are what the U.S. military would assign to its Special Ops forces if they issued motorcycles. They speak eloquently, if silently, on the subject of extremity; each motorcycle succinctly describes the future. And it is one, apparently, full of urgent needs, all of them taken into account. Thus, the bikes are lavishly wired and welded and stickered and accessorized and packed and rethought. They are prayers in the form of motorized vehicles, each clause and syllable carefully considered, now ready to be launched godward. They will go tomorrow, or wait patiently forever. But in fact it is only one more day before they will be asked to head out, and keep going for eleven days, on the twenty-fifth anniversary of the original endurance-motorcycling test.

The Iron Butt Rally is the mother of all rallies (in every sense of that word, but in the most untoward of them giving rise, during the past decade or so of an unprecedented flowering of rally fever, to dozens of smaller rallies: twelve, twenty-four, thirty-six hours; five days, ten days; the Utah 1088; the Minuteman 1K; the Butt Buster; the Minnesota 1000; the Raw-Hide; the Butt Lite; the Mason-Dixon 20–20; the You're Not Superman Rally; the Bally Rally in Ireland; long-distance runs in Finland and Russia, around England). But every mother has a grandmother, so the genealogy of the urge to go great distances in a specified time winds back to the birth of the internal combustion engine, which seems to have something in it that makes people want to run it, and themselves, to the final inch of valor, or throw valves trying. The teens and twenties saw innumerable cross-country runs and air derbies, meant to try machine and mettle. Then, starting in 1971, the Cannonball Run, an automotive race across the United States from Atlantic to Pacific, gave a man named Mike Rose, a motorcycle-industry *macher*, a little idea.

The two-day New York–to–San Francisco ride had been achieved. In the strange way of human thinking, the next thing must now be thought of, immediately. Then the next. Until finally there's the brick wall through which no one can pass: the far reach of physical possibility. This is what the endurance-riding institution now does for a pastime: conceive of something more difficult as soon as someone has just driven himself ragged doing the previously thought undoable. And so, in 1984, Rose wondered: Could one ride a circuit of the lower 48 in ten days? The Ironman triathlon was a popular event—people loved the idea of watching others beating themselves silly for no apparent good reason—so motorcyclists with certifiable "Ironbutts," as he put it, ought to be worth a gasp or two, not to mention a higher profile for motorcycling and sales of assorted gear (Rose's main business objective). To reel them in, the original poster foregrounds "scheduled" prize money of $40,000, purportedly offered by a variety of companies. (Most of the money never materialized, only an accumulated $500 from entry fees.) Ten riders entered, one of them backed by *Cycle Guide* magazine. Leaving from Montgomeryville Cycle Center in Philadelphia, riders were to check in at points in the four corners of the United States, and otherwise to ride hell for leather. They were required to fix their own bikes if something broke, and they were required to complete the ride with the same tires on which they started, an unwise idea that demanded direct negotiations with the devil: ride slowly and preserve rubber, or ride to win and risk safety.

Several riders that year managed the delicate give-and-take with their master from down below; there was a four-way tie for first place, something that would become an impossibility with a retooling of the competition's structure, into a sort of scavenger hunt, the next year. In 1985, there were twenty-five entrants, all invited.

By 1988, there were none. Not enough interest.

Enter Mike Kneebone, a software engineer from Chicago, who had exclusive rights to a magic elixir that transformed an event and subsequently brought forth a new sport from nothingness into unstoppable popularity. Perhaps he did not know this; perhaps he was simply a spirit possessed. Indeed, he had to be driven by something inexplicable to ride straight into the Guinness World Records three times: New York to San Francisco in forty-seven hours, forty-one minutes; the twenty-four-hour high-mileage record (1,707); hitting all forty-eight contiguous U.S. states in six days, thirteen hours, twenty-one minutes. (As proof of the assertion that long-distance riding is meant primarily to beget more long-distance riding, Kneebone is happy to note that his records have fallen: the first to Ken Hatton, who crossed the country by bike in forty-one hours; the

THE MAN WHO WOULD STOP AT NOTHING

third to Ron Ayres, in six days flat.) It hardly needed saying, but Kneebone said it anyway: "Riding is my life."

He had become involved in 1986, cofounding an association bearing the Iron Butt name, but he did not exert full power, including the use of his formidable marketing skills, until he took on the role of president (though "emperor" might be more precise, due to the organization's Napoleonic progress through the world, annexing and amassing members, certified rides, foreign branches, and even a business partner in "extreme ride" touring). After the rally's cancellation in 1988, he did some canny reconceptualizing before launching it again. First, he took prize money off the table, a move he believes has had a purifying effect on the event and has ensured its continued existence; paradoxically, the high entry fees borne by the participants themselves—the entry cost for 2009 was $1,850, exclusive of the endless costs run up before and during the rally itself—has deepened the pool of hopeful entrants. (This personal expense prompted a John Ryan quip that now appears on a revised edition of the *11 Days, 11,000 Miles* license-plate back: *11 Days, $11,000.*)

In 2009, about a thousand riders vied for a hundred spots, which were determined by lottery as well as by fiat of the emperor, who can make as many exceptions as he likes. This is to ensure "color" in the tint of bikes like the two vintage RE5 rotary-engine Suzukis from the seventies that were considered Hopeless Class entrants. They were also ones, this quarter of a century later, that were to give their reverent nod to rally history. That is because George Egloff was mounted on an RE5 when he rode to one of the first-place finishes in the original "Ironbutt" in 1984. Their inclusion in 2009 was the equivalent of placing a GEORGE WASHINGTON SLEPT HERE plaque on some old stone house; historical markers signify less the commemoration of a place than the legitimation of an institution. The Iron

Butt Rally was now officially a Big Event, wrapped in a corporate identity replete with sharp-minded legal counsel (Bob Higdon), an international following, two solid pages on trademarks and association history that go out to each person who becomes a member, and the voluminous storytelling—from multipart ride reports posted on blogs and forums to the official word of the organization in its daily reports during the rally and the articles in its new glossy magazine for "premier" members—that form Old and New Testaments of long-distance riding's Bible.

Besides, the underdog is an irresistible category in American self-conception. Motorcyclists may be disproportionately drawn to expressing humor of a dark sort. They are certainly fond of testing themselves, as witness the entire long-distance enterprise, so they are driven again and again to prove that Hopeless is sometimes not so hopeless after all, provided the rider on the underpowered machine has the guts to make up for the lack of displacement. The two smallest bikes ever to survive the crucifixion that is the Iron Butt Rally are 125s, Suzuki and Cagiva. The 2001 Hopeless Class was especially lively, with Paul Pelland finishing on a 2001 Russian-made Ural (which might as well have been a 1944 Ural) and, more heroically, a 1946 Indian Chief piloted by Leonard Aron making it all the way to the final checkpoint. In 2003, Leon Begeman came in twelfth on an EX250 Ninja that was actually resurrected from seven previously expired Ninjas. If kites were allowed in the Iron Butt Rally, someone would find a way to fireproof lightweight nylon and fit a four-valve engine to a balsa-wood frame. After flying seven feet above the ground for eleven days, the victor would crack jokes at the finishers' banquet while being good-naturedly jeered for stealing a top-ten place from someone who really deserved it.

To ensure the persistence of the rally into the future, its benevolent rulers peel back the blindfold from one eye to openly pull some chits from the bowl. They need to make sure the field contains a broad spectrum of rookie and seasoned; female; young and old; and foreign. Riders from English-speaking countries such as Australia, Canada, Ireland, and England will naturally have an advantage (so will entrants from countries such as Germany, where English is practically universal). The successful running of an endurance rally based on a bonus-points platform begins well before the bike is mounted. If you cannot read multipart instructions carefully, stacking every detail on top of its perfectly comprehended predecessor —and then repeat the process for each of hundreds of different bonuses, as well as for dozens of technical requirements—all the hard riding through nights and days will be for naught. Your fifth-grade composition teacher really was an important figure, after all. Among the snowfall of bonuses in the 2009 rally, one flake had five arms: phone in and give your name, your rider number, your current location, the last bonus you secured, and the next bonus you are headed for. One rider carefully complied with all the requirements when he made his call to score these points; the one thing he had overlooked was the fact that the time window for this bonus would not open until the next day. In the official account, it was reported that this gaffe made the rallymaster laugh so hard she began to cry. One wonders if the rider did the same, minus the laughter. Another rider, making the call during the appropriate time frame, knew that he was in a town called Keeler. He just did not know which state it was in.

The rally now takes place every two years; at its current level of professionalism, it could hardly occur more frequently, as neither organizers nor participants could prepare adequately in a single year. The motorcycles alone, standing in their patient line in the hotel parking lot, tell the story of meticulous preparation. Most of them have been outfitted with fuel cells, auxiliary gas tanks to carry as much extra fuel as permitted by rally rules; supplemental lights, often two sets (running lights for visibility and HID lights to brighten the night road); dual GPS units; antennas for radio or CB contact; hydration units—sometimes a watercooler drilled to accommodate a long tube of a straw and mounted in a welded rack behind or below the rider—custom seats, often covered with sheepskin or the ceramic Beadrider ventilation pad manufactured by one of the entrants; ports for electric-heated jackets and gloves; all manner of specially made mounts for bags and electronics and tools. They are packed as tightly as the space shuttle before a long orbit. And, since they are piloted by motorcyclists, they are individual. License plates read KEP ROLN; 1 PT; IBRO9 (there are two of those); IBRX2 (someone who's back for more); LDRIDER. One man has mounted laminated photos of his wife and children on the dash of his fairing as a sort of familial carrot dangling in front of him (the psychic stick is the knowledge that if he does something stupid, he will be doing it to them); another knows the tricks exhaustion and pressure can play on the memory, already reminding himself via stickers on his topcase: "Think!!"; "Date"; "Time"; "Location"; "Odometer"; "Gallons"; "Flag." Forgetting any one of these can mean a loss of points, and points is the whole point.

If you could boil down the ethos of long-distance endurance motorcycling at this, the pinnacle event (and you can't, because the eye pans like a movie camera across a thousand small details, each of which adds and confounds and complicates any simplification of the notion), it might, just might, be contained in the sticker adhering to the windshield of one of these bikes. "My local riding area," it says, over a map of the North American continent.

At the technical inspection the day before the start, odometers are checked with precision. Drivers are required to put the front wheel on a mark, then ride a specific and circuitous route back to the same spot; this "odometer check from hell" must be repeated by many before they get it right. Considering that it may be upwards of thirty miles, it is no small matter just before a major ride. And it will give riders the opportunity afterward to forget to disconnect every last one of the myriad electronic devices that festoon their bikes, and so, come morning and the figurative drop of the flag, some will not start. The discharged batteries will be cranked by bystanders' cars or bikes, and they will all get underway, eventually. The adventures start early, and stay up late, in this little game.

Other elements of the fine print before entry include the need to carry exceptionally comprehensive accident insurance and, in 2009 for the first time, MedJet injury coverage. In addition, the riders would be required to videotape an indemnification clearing the IBA of any blame, pass a Good Citizen decibel check of their exhaust systems, and attend two pre-rally seminars. One was presented by Don Arthur, MD, retired surgeon general of the U.S. Navy; behind him, a screen lit up at intervals with illustrations for his cautionary tales on the role of sleep in the body's functioning.* The graphs and charts and anatomical drawings flashed by as he explained how circadian rhythms must be attended to when planning naps on an endurance ride (setting the reprehensible clock known as a Screaming Meanie to go off in the period between forty-five minutes and two hours is a mistake; earlier or later is not), what to ingest and what not (nicotine decreases nighttime visual acuity by 30 percent; stimulants and energy drinks can be disastrous, but caffeine

---

* His knowledge of these effects comes also from that great medical school, the road. In 2002, he reportedly rode well over a hundred thousand miles.

can be useful as long as one has become acclimated to going without it for a period of time before it is needed—then, a cup of coffee can be taken when lying down for a nap, and thirty minutes later, when it has entered the bloodstream, it can act as a secondary, somewhat gentler, alarm). The most confounding facts that Arthur presented, however, involved the effects of sleep deprivation. Sleep cannot be banked to draw upon in times of poverty; the brain, like an overheated computer, needs to be shut off periodically. If it is not, strange things begin to happen. Speed begins to slow—mental circuits will no longer process external information at the rate they can when properly rested—and, particularly at night, the mind "fills in" perception gaps. Call it hallucinating. What is that series of lights elongating and changing height, coming right at you? *A single-engine plane—on the turnpike?* And then you're in the tunnel, and you know. You know how tired you are.

You might feel tired, but not that tired, as long as you stay on the bike, but the more devious truth shows itself when you roll to a stop. And forget to put your sidestand down. Or your feet. You are not just tired. You are pushing against exhaustion, and it is pushing back, ever stronger as you get weaker. That is the worst of these little bits of information showing on the PowerPoint screen, the very definition of irony: One of the seminal signs of fatigue is not recognizing how fatigued you are. So you think you do not need to stop, just yet. You will pass a gas station when you need fuel; you will find it hard to make decisions, usually choosing the simplest option, even when it is the worst. You will leave your rally towel hanging over the sign of the last bonus you visited—and not know it till the next bonus, four hundred miles down the road. Or you will leave all your receipts—those precious receipts! the prizes themselves, hard ridden for, hard won!—in an open pouch on the topcase, where, after a fuel stop, they proceed to vanish into the night, one after the other. The mistakes mount the longer the game goes on, and they can be costly, infuriating, and dangerous. Not that those who run the rally, or anyone in the Iron Butt establishment, likes to use that word, *dangerous*. But it hovers there, in the purified air of the Marriott bar, unspoken in the caesurae between jokes and ribbing and greetings and questions. The thing most feared is the nonthing: a microsleep, the moment when sleep takes you and you did not see it coming.

For juju against this hellhound, they'll stand on their pegs, or shake their heads, or sing loud songs. They'll raise their visors to get a blast of wind in the face, or make up lines of odd numbers and recite them forward and back. They'll take a sip of water and then expel it into the force of the wind, which sprays it back, a momentary cold shower.

Something about the Iron Butt, perhaps its grand scale, yields easily to the formation of aphorisms. "Stop to go farther." And if that doesn't speak to you, the next will: "No ride is worth your life." This is well understood, often repeated, and engraved in the consciousness of every rider who is serious enough to have attained membership in the IBA. They are arguably the most-skilled, best-trained motorcyclists on the planet. No property damage or injury to anyone but the riders themselves has ever occurred in the history of the rally. It would be an exercise in self-stupefaction to calculate miles per accident among them; but I would place all my money, and even my motorcycle, on a final number larger by far than any you would come up with by shaking the general riding population in the dice cup. The parking lot before any long-distance rally is a three-dimensional advertisement for Aerostich protective apparel; more than a thousand dollars of its gear goes by with nearly every bike that departs on the clock. Helmets are a stipulation of virtually every event, but they hardly need to be required, because few of these riders would dream of going a block, much less a thousand miles in a day, without one. They are the ones who believe in ATGATT as a precept of their religion: All The Gear All The Time. Period.

They also know that what they do is heavy with risk, even if they rarely speak of it, in the manner of the fighter-pilot fraternity as codified by Tom Wolfe—"that unspoken stuff" is so big it is never touched by the smallness of words.* Or maybe saying things brings them into being. So don't say anything. Don't worry, be happy. Life is for living. Rallies are for riding. But still, it happens. Some of the comrades they bunked with at extreme-riding boot camp—some of these same people who turn up in these hotel conference rooms, for the IBA's annual banquet during Bike Week in Florida, for any of the other dinners the night before the other rallies that now pepper the calendar, for any other excuse getting them together to ride separately—have in fact been taken down. When the rare and unthinkable happens, a shock radiates through the community: these larger-than-life characters, these fellows who knew without speaking what was in your head as you made the first turn out of a parking lot to face the long journey alone, or when you returned at

---

* Much of Wolfe's *The Right Stuff* speaks directly to long-distance motorcycling; where the words *fighter pilot* appear, simply substitute *LD rider*: "A fighter pilot soon found he wanted to associate only with other fighter pilots. Who else could understand the nature of the little proposition (right stuff/death) they were all dealing with? And what other subject could compare with it? It was riveting! To talk about it in so many words was forbidden, of course. The very words *death, danger, bravery, fear* were not to be uttered except in the occasional specific instance or for ironic effect. Nevertheless, the subject could be adumbrated in *code* or *by example*. Hence the endless evenings of pilots huddled together talking about flying."

last, four days of beard on your face and a wave of ecstasy cresting in your heart, they could not suddenly be gone, when just days before they were in their T-shirts and flip-flops and LD Comfort skivvies, poking around the wiring of a friend's bike to find an elusive short. The hollow-tipped bullets are exhaustion and deer. Almost every rider who has ever died in an Iron Butt Rally—three to date—was done in by these.

Sometimes—and this is the most chilling thing of all to the World's Toughest Motorcycle Riders—the one who goes is one of the best. Fran Crane undeniably was one of these. A close friend of Mike Kneebone, with whom she established a new record for riding through the lower 48 (6.6 days, in 1988), she had been a racer and a track coach. In the 1986 rally, she came in third; the next year, second. In that rally, she was the high-mileage finisher, with 12,166 miles over the eleven days. She was a formidable, talented rider. And in the 1999 rally, she crashed. It is probable that her saddlebag hit a guardrail, but it is also possible that the truth will never be known. It is also probable that her helmet, a modular style, got pulled into the error and malfunctioned where it was supposed to take a blow. But the truly unfathomable mistake was that of the nurse in the ICU, who chose exactly the wrong fluid—a blood thinner—and pumped it directly into the conscious woman's vein.

An unsolved mystery also surrounds the death of Ron Major in the 1997 rally. The photos are something out of that dream whose odd, impossible details you can't shake upon waking: a red Honda ST1100, propped up against a guardrail on the shoulder of the highway as if it were no weightier than a bicycle, its rider having seen an ice-cream stand and braked to a quick stop for a few moments. The motorcycle was not wrecked; the body of fifty-five-year-old Major, a dedicated long-distance motorcyclist and television technician, was found a quarter of a mile up the road from his bike. His family requested an autopsy, which they say revealed the cause of death as a massive coronary attack. Whether or not this would have occurred if he were mowing the lawn instead of engaging in a long-distance rally, no one can say. Nor can they explain any of the rest of this scenario, the one that will haunt the mind of anyone who goes out on a miserably long ride. Rallyers leaving the Yakima checkpoint after learning of Major's death were asked if they wanted to carry a reminder of their fellow competitor. Each one left on the next leg with a strip of memorial black tape on their windscreen.

In the 2009 rally, death will again appear, diving swiftly from the night sky and vanishing as quickly to leave only broken pieces of understanding. David "Davo" Jones, president of the Iron Butt Association of Australia and of the Australian distance group Far-Riders, which he founded, will cross back into the United States from Canada on an early September day near the end of the rally. And riders on the way to the final checkpoint in Spokane, Washington, will stop at the scene of an accident to see a strange and confounding sight.* Davo's helmet will be strapped to the back of his bike. He will have hit a deer and gone down, at a speed of about 45 mph. Helmets are compulsory in Australia. They are compulsory in the Iron Butt Rally. But Davo will not be wearing his, in the cold early morning in Idaho, at the moment a deer leaps across the road.

He is fifty-two; he has a wife and four children. His license plate reads GO FAR.

---

* The rules stipulate that a participant who fails to offer assistance to a fellow rider who is stopped, perhaps in need, will be disqualified, though it is hard to imagine that these brethren would need the requirement spelled out. More than one rider in more than one rally has lost his own chance at finishing because he went to the aid of another.

It is events such as these that make the second pre-rally seminar for entrants obligatory, and top secret. Only those with assigned numbers are allowed into the Marriott conference room to hear Bob Higdon address the matter of the media. Reporters looking for a sensational hook to their rally stories will press competitors to reveal that they are mischievous criminals, are pulling dangerous stunts on public roads, are insane (they may be) or a threat or accidents waiting to happen. They would love to paint a lurid word picture full of speed junkies racing across the map without care for law or limb.* These endurance riders, most of whom are focused on the job at hand, could naively say the wrong thing, which might then be ornamented enough to imply that the association is sanctioning, nay, encouraging, the breaking of speed limits while high on sleeplessness. But the association is sophisticated enough to cover itself with an indemnifying umbrella large enough for all the innocents who can crowd beneath it. The IBA has never published a record that can be found illegal by the division function on a calculator: the two-thousand-mile day becomes "over 1,500 miles" on the printed certificate, and then the doors shut. They will never open for the likes of the genial and soft-spoken ex–law-enforcement officer who, by his own tongue-in-cheek admission, "crossed from 'serve and protect' to 'public menace'" by one time accomplishing, just to see if he could, the feat of throttling a bike 2,245 miles in twenty-four hours. It was never, and never would be, sanctioned by the organization in any way. But do the division, and stare slack-jawed at the little

---

* In fact, rallyists (if not those who are gunning for a new record, a different breed) rarely if ever break the limit: the average speed of the past few winners of the Iron Butt Rally was between 45 and 48 mph. This is because the rally is not about speed—is in fact antithetical to speeding—but rather is about endurance coupled with routing suss.

numbers staring back from the digital screen. Then start feeling an uncomfortable sensation in the bottom of your stomach when you learn that the moving average over the first nine hours of that ride was 120 mph.

They must try what they can to protect what they do, this stealth activity that takes place in the public sphere but under the radar of public notice. It is fairly amazing that, in a time of unprecedented surveillance of virtually every activity, such large acts could be undertaken in plain sight. Just the credit-card trails alone, if read, would tell a stunning story. They are holding a great and private pleasure in their hands, the long-distance riders, and it could be taken away by the schoolmarms of legislation, those who increasingly run the world. Though, it occurs to me, the lack of revenue-generation for a governmental entity truly poses the greatest threat to the endeavor, for that which makes no money for anyone is not long for this world anymore.

In a certain light, it is amazing that only three deaths have occurred during Iron Butt events. Injuries have occurred, certainly. So, to ward off more, you must invoke the spirits of Perverse Irony and give them a burnt offering: "We're okay as long as we only off our own," grimly jokes an insider, "but the first time one of us takes out the bus full of Girl Scouts, we're done for."

It seems so unlikely. Yes, but so does the accident on a sunny day when you've just decided to run to the grocery store on the bike instead of in the car. I know. I know. Yet it is impossible to watch this group of motorcyclists, with their cumulative millions of miles, so terribly serious and knowledgeable and quietly skilled, and not think, *Not them. They are not of this world, and they are not prone to its laws of breakage.* Here's the slogan that formed itself in my head, after hearing from John Ryan that those twenty-eight bone fractures belonged solely to his early riding career, not a one occurring after he joined the ranks of long-distance endurance riders: "Join the Iron Butt Association and Stay Safe!"

If this were the case, however, the air the next morning would not have been so dense with the molecules of all the emotions that had been emitted by the riders who now stood by their motorcycles, helplessly looking them over. The hour was too late for any second guesses. At the banquet the previous night, they clutched their just-received bonus packets—the only map to the Holy Grail they sought as devotedly as questing knights, and wearing as much armor.

The theme of this year's bonuses, 334 of them across forty-nine states and six Canadian provinces, had been conceived by Bob Higdon and bore the deep impress of his peculiar attorney's view of the general run of humanity (not terribly esteemed, except for the creative stupidity of which it seems endlessly capable). He had had his fun with them, and soon it would be the riders' turn. Finally the omnipresence of yellow crime-scene tape as a decorative element in the rally poster and the neck ribbons holding the competitors' badges was explained: They were to visit locations of America's most notorious (and sometimes most absurd) crimes. They could collect bonus points by going to Washington, DC, and photographing their bikes in front of spy Kim Philby's home; they could visit the site of the massacre of Cheyenne Indians, at Sand Creek, in Colorado; they might opt to ride to Louisiana to snap a quick photo of the stone marker at the spot where Bonnie and Clyde met their bloody ends. They were not, however, unless they were patently insane, to attempt the "sucker bonus," the high-point, difficult-to-bag location placed on the list primarily for the amusement of the rally staff. Mike Kneebone, from the podium while a hundred nervous eaters finished dinner, implored them not to try it. He knew, of course, that many would; he expected them to, would have been disappointed in his followers had they not leapt high from the water to gracefully steal the bait from his sharp hook. ("Basically, for eleven days, you're our little puppet," Kneebone explains with unsuppressed glee in a 2007 interview in *Hard Miles*, a documentary on the rally.)

The site of this forbidding, and alluring, bonus was where Edward Kennedy in 1969 had driven his car off the causeway to Chappaquiddick Island, killing Mary Jo Kopechne but failing to report the death for many hours. And it was worth a mouthwatering 6,652 points.

The small difficulty with the bonus was not the fact that it was 950 miles from the start. It was not even that you can't make reservations for motorcycles on the ferry to Martha's Vineyard; it is first come, first served, and many, many people wish to be served in August, at one of the East Coast's premier vacation destinations. It was that the island was effectively in lockdown, due to the almost simultaneous arrival of two very different disruptions: President Barack Obama and his family, and Hurricane Bill.

It would be folly to attempt it. Besides, there were 123 other first-leg bonuses to choose from before having to pull in at the first checkpoint in St. Charles (not to mention the "simple" need to chew up that extensive mileage to Illinois).

It must have been an irrepressible attraction to folly, then— perhaps the very essence of the rally—that made twenty-three riders, including every one of the top ten as of the scorecard in St. Charles, go to Martha's Vineyard. One of them was Jim Owen, a "routing master" whose motorcycle finally decided to get with the plan and finish with its rider. In the 2003 rally, the alternator belt had snapped on his BMW R1200RT, leaving him in seventy-sixth place; in 2005, he led the field until twelve hours before the finish, at which time his final drive cashed in its chips. He was given a rare standing ovation at the finishers' banquet, which did nothing to repair either his final drive or his intense frustration, but perhaps acted as the aspirin of collegial sympathy. In 2007, he came in second. He was overdue for his 2009 win, which he would take with 139,833 points.

• • •

THERE ARE so many bonus waypoints that, when input, a small colored flag representing each one, the map of North America turns an almost impenetrable red. The bonuses are this year for the first time delivered to contestants by memory sticks that can upload the waypoints directly into GPS units via mapping software. (The high percentage of IT careers among the entrants was either the chicken or the egg in the continuing technologizing of the rally.)* This does not mean that choosing a route is automatic, or easy. A brain with the extra convolutions to formulate a winningly smart route—"Plan your ride, and ride your plan"—is a gift one can only be born with, like the legs that can perform a *grand jeté* to Kirov Ballet standards. The complexities of doing so are mathematical, physical, geographical, and imaginative all at once. Above that, above even the per-

---

* A German named Martin Hildebrandt first used GPS in a rally in 1995. Now it is inconceivable to ride a rally—unless it is one of the few nostalgic rallies conducted the old-fashioned way—using paper maps. We have the U.S. military to thank for Big Brother's assistance, in the form of twenty-eight satellites launched beginning in 1978, to circle unseen above us, seeing all. We are found, and we are thus lost. Yet while some riders will no longer leave home without them, others use GPS only to get home: they ride where they like, turning down the unknown lanes that often prove to be rubies among the garnets of usual roads. When the time comes, they turn on the GPS to find home.

severance to push beyond the exhaustion and frustration that can, and do, make grown men cry, over all the talent and intelligence and conditioning and will, hangs luck. Like a cloud that either shields you from a hot sun or breaks open in catastrophes of gray thunder. Mechanical failure, like the deer, waits in the shadows to dart suddenly into the roadway.

It has lately been waiting largely for the final drives of late-model BMWs.

These Bavarian bikes have long been the preeminent marque among endurance riders, but reliability is the man you marry in long-distance riding, not loyalty to the brand. Four final drives of BMWs expired in the 2007 rally, and this was reflected in the choice of mounts in 2009 (as well as the decisions of two BMW riders, Jeff Earls and Ken Meese, to carry one additional expensive and heavy spare part in their kits: final-drive units). Most major manufacturers were well represented, with the exception of Harley; only one was entered.* Hondas proved extremely popular, with a total of twenty GL1800 Gold Wings in the lineup, eleven ST1300s, and three ST1100s; in addition, there were nineteen Yamaha FJR1300s, while Kawasakis carried five riders. But old habits, and loves, die hard. BMWs placed first, second, fourth, and fifth in the 2007 rally; in 2009, notwithstanding the ominous threat of breakdown, they would take first, second, and fourth. In all, thirty-four riders would stand by their BMWs, whether touring, sport-touring, or dual-purpose

---

* Tom Austin's official ride report for the day before the rally was full of the statistics that endurance riding sloughs off like skin cells: "Harley, which has about 30 percent of the highway motorcycle market in the U.S., is the choice of only one rider," while BMW, with "about one percent of the U.S. market, is the choice of 35 percent of the riders." He explains the reasons: "The ergonomics of most Harley models are all wrong for long distance comfort and the company doesn't enjoy the same reputation other brands have in the areas of handling, braking, reliability, and performance."

models. One of them would be an R60/6 that had stood by its rider too, for thirty-three years and more than 500,000 miles.

The memory of BMW's dearly departed longevity was saluted in the first bonus, an easy pot of golden points that nearly every rider would head for the second the clock started ticking at ten on Monday morning, August 24. The factory in Greer, South Carolina, was the first yellow-tape scene to visit. The crime committed here was "failure to keep making one of the more reliable Iron Butt motorcycles ever built," and the bonus was secured by taking a picture of said bike on display: Ed Culberson's 1981 R80G/S, "Amigo." In 1985–86, it became the first vehicle to traverse nearly the entire length of the Western Hemisphere, including the perilous Darien Gap.

This bonus was listed as worth 666 points.

The combination of high points and an eighteen-mile distance from the start meant that almost all the riders routed themselves by way of Greer, and the visitors' center was mobbed. Of course, the rally organizers could not have anticipated, or desired, such a thing. No. Of course not.

•  •  •

IN 2005, John Ryan, a rookie, ran the Iron Butt Rally. Bob Higdon wrote of his performance:

> Like a number of the top flight people in the endurance riding community, Ryan can display moments of genius and moments of unbelievable stupidity. . . . He screwed up the first two legs of the event so badly that we were actually laughing at him by the time the third (and final) leg started. Then he climbed over fifteen people on that final leg to finish seventh overall. It's one thing to jump from 100th place to 85th because you're just put-

*ting losers behind you, but to leapfrog over the best riders in the rally is an entirely different matter. The IBR is about pure endurance, but there aren't three better endurance tales in its storied history than Ryan's last four days in 2005.*

Ryan says he will never run another rally. Unless he can do it on a pre–World War II BMW. Then the playing field will be leveled. And he can return the rally to what it was: about one rider, the road, and the will to go on. No mapping program can help you on that ride. Ryan wants no help. Only to be left alone, to go.

• • •

**MONDAY MORNING DAWNS** sunny and warm, ideal for the beginning of an epic both useless and so deeply meaningful it cracks the brain to fathom it; both bold and foolhardy. When these hundred riders now milling around their motorcycles with anticipation's knuckles white around their guts leave the parking lot of the Marriott, they will be going to more places than crime scenes spread across the United States of America, which may well be the crime capital of the world. They will be going to elemental places within themselves. Elemental places on our anthropological timeline, too, it turns out.

Bob Lilley, a rally rookie who would finish eighth and report that at the end of leg two, with one more to go, "I just didn't give a shit if I missed any easy 'on-the-way' bonii. I was mentally and physically spent," had given up booze for three months before the rally. He lost eight pounds during the rally. Two days before the end, he lost his dopp kit, which he admitted had only been used intermittently, and now "just 'scraped the fur' off my teeth with teriyaki beef jerky and then ate it when I was done."

Of the 101 riders who started, seventy would finish. One would die. Those thirty who otherwise did not finish would be done in by the clock, mechanical failure, illness, the always variable "personal reason," and, perhaps, an inability to stare down the miles and not blink. There are many miles, and only one of you.

Only 364 people had ever finished an Iron Butt Rally before this; as Kneebone points out, that is fewer humans than have been shot into outer space in rockets.

It is so crushing an undertaking that no rider has ever led the rally from start to finish. It is so brutal a journey that everyone who goes on it is never again the same.

I had spent two days watching a pageant whose import I had not yet begun to comprehend. The players do not know I'm watching, trying to locate the source of the strange mix of awe and longing that rotates in my skull. I am still trying to understand.

I sit on a bench outside the sliding glass doors of the ostensibly elegant Marriott, holding an unread copy of *USA Today*; they are cut from the same corporate, peculiarly uniform American cloth. I watch the bikes come and go. A moment like a film clip, an unknown subject passing through the frame, unaware that he is observed. Wondered at. But he is, and I do. The modular helmet, flipped up; a quick head check, looking right then left, focused, absorbed by what is immediate: the Aerostich suit; the aluminum bags. The soundtrack is the satisfying bite of metal to metal as first gear is engaged with a satisfying *chunk*; then the low growl as the throttle compels the machine to move, the rider to weight the handlebar so the bike dips low to the right in a graceful turn. Then he is gone, on a mission that is private, like all the moments we spend on our motorcycles. You don't need to know.

That is why I need to know. All the accoutrements I note, all the attitude, telegraph that these people mean business. That concentration and sense of purpose are more appealing than any rare cologne could ever be. That is when it strikes me all over again: *Motorcycling is goddamn* cool. When done with this much proficiency and mastery, *stone* cool.

The very essence of cool, of course, is life grabbed with no intermediary. A moment lived so fully there is no room to worry what is beyond it. And, as one competitor told me after a minute's consideration the previous night in the bar, the reason he rides is to feel alive.

At 8:30 a.m. on a late-August day in 2009, the final technical checks begin. Final GPS checks. Orange stickers placed on windshields, to indicate the OK. Neck cards punched. Failsafe after failsafe. The riders whose goals are simply to finish look relaxed; the ones who are looking to place—which is as much as saying, "to win," although such a thing is rarely said, as they don't sell a voodoo charm to ensure winning something that has so many variables no human could truly control them all—have their grim game faces on. The young man who spoke the previous night about feeling alive on his bike suddenly isn't doing so well: he is second-guessing the first-leg route he has chosen. He looks constricted by doubt.

The chief technical inspector, Dale "Warchild" Wilson, addresses the waiting crowd through a bullhorn. Wilson, if only by virtue of a demeanor with three words in its vocabulary—"Don't cross me"—italicized by his Fu Manchu mustache, makes everyone listen. This is important. This is minutes to the end of the waiting that has lasted two years. These are the final instructions, three of them. His voice rings out clear through the amplifier: "Finish. Stay safe. And do not embarrass this organization." He waits a half beat: "Repeat. *Do not embarrass this organization.*"

And then they start their bikes.

At the sound, my stomach lurches. In a precise choreography,

Wilson waves them out alternately, nose to tail, from two oppos-ing lines of bikes. Some take the turn out of the parking lot gin-gerly: these are the ones to whom appeared a blood-chilling vision of dropping their bikes on a slow-speed maneuver in front of the IBA president, his rallymaster (the beautiful and cunning Lisa Landry), the multitudinous staff and volunteers, a television crew, a videog-rapher, and all the onlookers, such as the far-flung members of the Motorcycle Tourer's Forum, here, in the words of one of them, like "groupies to the world's biggest rock concert." They put their feet down as insurance, however, primarily against embarrassment before their own cohort, the other entrants, the riders they will both be with and riding to best.

In no more than ten minutes, a hundred and one riders are gone. We who are left behind stand there before the emptiness of asphalt. The silence is stunning. Part of us—our sinews, perhaps, or our hearts—has stretched as far along the road after them as it can go, and just before breaking in two has returned, sagging. Now the competitors are alone on their journey. It will take them to so many places, not all of which are on the bonus list they carry.*

It is a curious feeling, after I have ridden home to New York from South Carolina, to feel my own thousand-mile day begin to recede into the past, day by day more distant. It is more curious still, like hearing a faraway bell without knowing from where or why it tolls, to suddenly remember, a week later, that they are still out there, riding the roads of America through the dark and the days. It haunts me for a week. I have returned to routine life, and later, changed for-ever, so will these once-ordinary women and men.

---

* In 2007, these were printed on red paper so they could not be faxed to an illegal, out-side, accomplice.

**Pause**

## THEY ENDURE

Of the quest to conquer Annapurna, to be the first climbers to top a mountain of 8,000 meters, which cost two of them (Maurice Herzog and Louis Lachenal) all their toes, and one of them his fingers too, it was written:

> *Presently, of course, someone asked the inevitable question. "Was it worth it?"*
>
> *Herzog's only answer was a smile. It was a needless question. To him and to his companions of course it was worth it. This is the story of brave men. Some may think it is also a story of foolhardy men. But if nothing else, it demonstrates that there are still among us those who are willing to struggle greatly for wholly ideal ends; for whom security is not the be-all and end-all of living; for whom there are conquests to be won in the world other than over their fellow men.*
>
> —"Annapurna," *Life*, July 9, 1951

•

In 1916, Ruth Bancroft Law set the American record for cross-country flight by flying a Curtiss biplane 511 miles nonstop from Chicago to Hornell, New York, and then on to New York City, in eight hours, fifty-five minutes, and twenty-five seconds.

(She also set an altitude record of 11,200 feet.) She was the first woman authorized to wear a military uniform, in 1917, yet she was denied permission to serve in combat.

•

A Swiss-Argentine by the name of A. F. Tschiffely, around 1929, began a two-and-a-half-year journey on horseback from the tip of South America to Washington, DC. The critics were immediately on him: "Most of the papers thought the trip was impossible and one or two said frankly that I ought to consult a doctor," he said.

When he arrived in New York, his return to Argentina was delayed by an official reception, causing him to miss his sailing on the *Vestris*, which sank with more than a hundred lives lost. Many of them presumably had been leery of attempting such a dangerous adventure as his.

•

John Glenn's "Project Bullet" of 1957 saw him flying from California to New York in a blazing three hours, twenty-three minutes, and 8.4 seconds, a transcontinental record of 725.55 mph. The future astronaut chose the name because he would fly faster than a .45-caliber bullet. After refueling, he flew as high as 50,000 feet.

•

Extreme skier Kristen Ulmer, the first woman to make a descent of Grand Teton, analogizes extreme athletics this way: "It's one thing to be a really good basketball player, but imagine if every time you missed a basket, somebody would shoot you in the head. It would be a lot more exciting, right?"

•

Jennifer Figge, of Aspen, Colorado, in 2009 swam 2,160 miles of the Atlantic Ocean over twenty-four straight days, attempting to reach the Bahamas from the Cape Verde Islands. Waves as high as thirty feet and strong winds prevented her from reaching her destination. The first man to swim across the Atlantic was Benoit Lecomte of France, who in 1998 swam 3,716 miles over seventy-three days without a kickboard from Cape Cod to Brittany.

.

Dean Karnazes ran 350 miles—in eighty hours—without sleep.

.

In the Tour d'Afrique, an annual 12,000-kilometer bicycle race from Cairo to Cape Town, participants spend 120 days, ninety-six of those riding, at a rate of 125 kilometers per day.

.

In a Cessna 174 (which now hangs from the ceiling of McCarran International Airport in Las Vegas), Robert Timm and John Cook flew continuously from December 4, 1958, to February 7, 1959. Their flight ended only because their engine did: after constant running, it could no longer regain altitude after flying low to refuel from a truck in the Mojave Desert. Still, the pilots admitted that sleeping in four-hour shifts had become deeply problematic long before the engine died. Their record still stands.

.

In 1966, after an eight-hour climb of El Capitan in Yosemite National Park, two twenty-six-year-olds named Mike Pelkey and Brian Schubert jumped from the top and parachuted down, creating a new sport that would be termed BASE jumping. On landing, Schubert claimed that he "heard every bone in both feet break." On the fortieth anniversary of his first extreme jump, he attempted the 876-foot drop from a bridge over the New River Gorge in West Virginia while 145,000 people watched. His parachute failed, and he died on impact with the water. His onetime partner said of him, "He was the poster boy of fearlessness."

# 4. A circle back

Something old, something new; something borrowed,
something blue.

—WEDDING CUSTOM

Tempus edax rerum.
[Time destroys everything.]

—OVID

**ON A HILL IN THE BERKSHIRES,** in front of our friends and families,
the words were spoken. Fifteen years later, they were unspoken. My
marriage was over. It was not a tragedy, although it was our tragedy.

In the interim, I had fallen into a long sleep in which motorcycles appeared only in vague and unsettling dreams. I left bikes, but,
as I was to learn, they had not left me. On the flyleaf of the book I
had given to the new owner of my motorcycle before he took it away
forever, I wrote, "Take care of a very special bike—you'll know why.
And ride your heart out!"

Instead of riding motorcycles, a few years into married life, I did other things. We got a puppy. Then another dog. A baby boy was born. A new house was bought in a new place. New friends were made. New books were written.

Late one night in the small office of the house I had rented after the big house was sold, all the possessions laboriously dispersed to the Salvation Army, to friends, to Freecycle, to yard sales, to a storage facility, I went on a procrastinatory journey through the unknowable spaces that always open behind the blue screen of the computer. The boy slept upstairs. I did not know where I was going. I left-clicked.

"Moto Guzzi 1100 Sport (ride in the montain)" opened across the screen. I turned the dial on the speaker. Suddenly, an engine rumble, familiar, like home. Up through the gears, downshift, upshift. The image was unfocused and shook, but the sound swelled forth perfectly, richly. It grew, reverberating, until it erupted inside, like it was part of blood and bone. I was no longer hearing it; it was coming from inside me. The song concentrated at the level of the chest. Later, I thought, *Isn't that strange? The place the heart resides.* But then, all I knew was that, this evening in the dark of autumn in upstate New York, a mystery occurred. As if I was split in two *(I was)*, I watched the person next to me. Tears collected in her eyes, then spilled down her face. She was utterly surprised. She did not know the ability to be moved by the simple fact of *a motorcycle* had lain there, still alive, after all this time. I do not think these tears were of sadness, not anymore. It was the music. All that it signified. She was crying at pure beauty, the great, moving sound of a big V-twin.

I had thought motorcycles were behind me. In that moment I knew they were, instead, before me.

· · ·

**ON JULY 14, 2008,** John Ryan wrote me an e-mail.

> We were introduced by Bob Higdon at the 2006 Square Route
> Rally.
>
> At the end of your presentation, we spoke about what it would
> take to get you started riding again, and may have exchanged
> e-mail addresses so that I might find a way to encourage you.

We did? I had no recollection. Then, motorcycles were still behind
me. Now, a mere twelve months later, I had no way to keep anything from anywhere. It all spilled, floated, crashed, waves before
me, around. Even my skin was torn away. There was no defense I
could use, and no separation between what had been me and what
wanted to get at me. I had cried for a year—in the car, washing the
dishes, on the shoulders of friends and family, on the phone, at my
fiftieth birthday party, walking the dog, watching a cartoon, writing
e-mails, to the clerk at Trader Joe's, on the plane to Ohio for Christmas, packing up the attic, in the shower, in the middle of the night. I
had not known it was possible to cry so much without being turned
inside out, to die from it.

I politely declined his invitation to a gathering of bikers at his
home in New Jersey. Muttfest, he called it. ("2. No loud pipes. If
it isn't stock, it's loud. Drive your car instead.") Six months later,
another e-mail landed in my in-box.

> Make getting back on a motorcycle as high a priority as possible.
>
> It will begin with your will, so let's start there. You need to
> immerse (okay, we'll start with wading in) yourself in motorcy-
> cling. Attend the NY motorcycle show (when was the last time
> you went?).

Indeed, when? Why, it was back in that other life, the one before this last one, which now lay shipwrecked on a shoal just off the beach. I surveyed the hull sticking up from the lapping water; even I was getting sick of looking at its broken boards.

But I was not sick of offering excuses.

. . . And don't expect me to let you give up on it so easily. There will always be many more obstacles than reasons.

Who was this tenacious person, and why did he think that getting back on a motorcycle could fix everything, even a complicated life that contained a dog, a temporary home with life in boxes stored at several spots around the county, work for which there was no longer any will, and especially an eight-year-old boy?

I am certainly glad to help, but the only appropriate thanks will be to make sure you complete your return to motorcycling and start getting some good miles, and the good life that goes with them, soon.

To the protest that until I found a house, I would not know how much money, if any, I could devote to buying a bike—well, he had a simple solution for that, too.

Hmmm . . . that's reasonable, but you need to be on a motor-cycle within three months. If you have a psychiatrist, have a prescription written, and get your health insurance to pay for it.

Ha! This was no ordinary booster, like my friends offering their ideas on what I could do (move back to New York City! join Match.com!

take a teaching job! take a vacation! meet their husband's recently divorced friend! come out for a drink on Friday night! stop thinking about myself so much! do more yoga! live in a mobile home while building a house! join Match.com!). This was someone who put his head down to push his full weight against a problem until it simply gave way. On the other side, there was a motorcycle. In every event, a motorcycle.

You won't need doors and windows until the winter, anyway. Or, you can get a mortgage that's $3K bigger. Small sacrifice for the love of your life, don't you think?

I was weakening. I was starting to think out loud about how I could justify the expense. There was a distant light, and I wanted to see what it was. I wanted to walk toward it, out of the darkness. "I want a bike," I finally wrote.

Everyone should, but most don't deserve one.

So when I ran out of rejoinders to John Ryan, I bought a ticket to the motorcycle show and took the bus down to Manhattan. I walked the long, cold January blocks to the Javits Center and went in.

. . .

**I HAD KEPT** a box with my remaining gear—my helmet, my jacket, my trickle charger. There was my tank bag, too, with the tire gauge and the spark-plug socket that fit only a ghost motorcycle. The box had lived in a closet in Brooklyn, then moved, unopened, to the attic of a Victorian farmhouse a hundred miles north. Eight years later, I looked at it only briefly before sending it to storage, along with all the books I thought I would not need, and the Christmas decorations. I knew I would have a house before Christmas. I had to.

In March, Ryan wrote that there was a BMW K75 for sale on consignment at a shop near him. He knew these mile-eating bikes: he had ridden his for two hundred thousand miles. It had taken him not only the 12,573 miles of the Iron Butt Rally, but also allowed him to become the first rider to complete a thousand-mile day totally within the limits of a city, when in May 2006 he did eighty-eight laps of a 16.3-mile route within Washington, DC (1,438 miles in less than twenty-four hours). He wrote in a message that a K75 was the only bike ever to finish the New York City 1000 (five months after the Washington ride), 1,216 miles achieved in eighty laps of a 15.2-mile course, "and the guy didn't even take the saddlebags off." "The guy" turned out to be John Ryan.

He had worn down my protests like sandpaper smooths off a sharp edge. Or, rather, he issued a challenge, which is hard to turn from when the obdurate John Ryan is issuing it and when you are the kind of person who deep down fears at all moments she may be that most pathetic of creatures, the one not up to a challenge. It was part seduction, part command: *Buy a bike . . . Buy a* bike*!*

And after I'd jumped off the cliff when he said, "Jump!" not knowing all that would unfold—that knowledge would in fact dawn slowly, over time, and take me to surprise, anger, disgust, peace, elation, and detachment in due course—I realized he had given me a gift. It was one that perhaps only he could give: pushed by force into a state of grace.

•  •  •

**IN APRIL,** I swung my leg over a blue K75. Ryan was watching as I rode it slowly down the gravel drive of a rented house. Out on the pavement, the bike slipped smoothly into second gear, and I could not stop smiling. How could I have forgotten what this was like, this melting into being? The stirrings of an emotion I no longer recognized were surfacing: happiness, in its essential, pure state. I don't think I had smiled at anything other than my son, and meant it, for almost two years.

I was smiling even more when I rode back up the drive: this short ride had been like a promise, one that you know will be kept. I liked that kind of promise. I slowed, banking right so I could turn left under the shed roof and onto the sheet of plywood we had found in the old barn out back to form a solid parking base on top of the thick gravel. I couldn't stop grinning. Then I pulled in the clutch. That's when I found myself standing over my new bike, my legs on either side and it now lying on its right side. How could this be? Shock immobilized me. Ryan ran. He flipped the kill switch. Oh, that's what I needed to remember: when you drop your bike, Melissa, remember to hit the kill. I filed this away. It was a new time, and you needed new knowledge for it.

A corer had gone through me, and emptiness now ran the length of my being. I had dropped a bike, under power, for the first time. The words I had read recently—*The K75 is a supremely reliable, smooth-running motorcycle, reputed to be one of the best BMW has ever built, but it has a tendency to be top-heavy*—came back to me. What had I done? The Lario had never done anything like this. I don't recall ever feeling that I couldn't do anything, go anywhere, on it: U-turns, the sloping grass at a rally site, parking lots of every type. My fears from the Italian past had all centered on *What will I do on that dark road late at night when it suddenly becomes the Bartleby the Scrivener of motorcycles: "I prefer not to run."* My fears were never: *Can I turn around without keeling over?*

I felt that I might be engaged in a fatal charade, not confronting the inimical changes time had slyly pushed toward me when I wasn't looking: grocery bags felt a little heavier now, putting boxes up on the top shelf sometimes impossible. The insidious laughter of the reading glasses, at home in the desk drawer as if they were not necessary now in almost every situation, or at least the ones requiring perusal of a menu in dim light or the ingredients list on every other product in the store.

I had fretted about this ever since receiving those e-mails, the ones that made me ask myself, *Will I? Should I? Could I?*

As usual, Ryan had an answer.

As you know, there are no guarantees, but good skills are the closest we will get to having one. Reflexes slow very gradually, they're a survival instinct. Pour boiling water on a centenarian's hand and he will smack you with his cane before you can see it.

Perhaps. But then, he *is* on a cane.

I felt ready for a cane myself. Or, at the least, remedial riders ed.

The things you think you're going to have to deal with, the things you lie in bed enumerating and attempting to solve, are the things that will never occur. The things you could never have dreamed in a hundredscore nights of dreams—those are the things that will become your Waterloo.

Better start arming. The enemy masses now on the other side of the field.

· · ·

**A DAY LATER** found me in New Jersey. We had ridden two-up on the K75 back to Ryan's home in western New Jersey, in the middle of horse country. It was odd indeed to see the sprawling mansion in which he lived with two of his sisters and his brother-in-law: a 5,500-square-foot Palais de Trop lacking nothing aside from its own helipad. (The neighborhood had in fact recently banded together to shut down plans for a private landing area nearby, since that level of activity represented a bridge too far for even these denizens of Indulgenceville.) On riding up the drive, he had turned back to his pillion to observe, "Not bad for an unemployed man, eh?"

Ryan had decided that the next ride he must take on was the Ultimate Coast to Coast: Prudhoe Bay, Alaska, above the Arctic Circle, to the tip of Key West, Florida. The record for the 5,645 miles stood at ninety-six hours, a time Ryan felt sure he could best by a considerable margin, notwithstanding the 101 hours it had taken him the previous year. ("If I could have turned around at the finish and gone back to do it again, I would have.") The dreadful conditions at the top of the Haul Road (aka Dalton Highway)—more than four hundred miles of rain, snow, abysmal fog, and even worse road conditions—had thrown a wrench into the starting time's works; by the time the weather had cleared sufficiently to depart, the lack of proper food while the rider sat at the ready, waiting, had caused a blood-sugar crisis. If this time he was more careful, and just a bit luckier, he knew he could take this record down to the mat. Records are sacrosanct in the IBA—if it belongs to your friend, you leave it there on the wall. But the record of someone not so well loved— place a target over it and go grease your gun.

The problem was that Ryan, being essentially unemployed except for occasional gigs as a bar bouncer and motorcycle marshal at New York City triathlons and road races, had nowhere to lay his hands on the $10,000 or more it would take to complete the run. Four sets of tires would be shredded along the way, by rock and gravel and the unduly high temperature of continuous running. Four oil changes; $1,700 for gas; usurious motel rates in Alaska; another three thousand miles just to get to the starting line. And so on. His FJR would have 130,000 miles on it when it reached Prudhoe, and more than a few of the essential moving parts already required attention. Throwing himself on the mercy of fellow motorcyclists was the only possible course of action.

A benefit lunch was planned at a Middle Eastern restaurant in New Brunswick, New Jersey. Ryan promised to accompany me back to upstate New York afterward. Apart from an hour's private reacquaintance lesson from a Motorcycle Safety Foundation instructor in a college parking lot, on a 250, I had ridden a total of about forty miles since stopping eleven years earlier. I had yet to find my sea legs.

Ponying up a hundred dollars each, the partygoers talked motorcycles and ate stuffed grape leaves. But when the appointed time came after the benefit, Ryan realized he could not spare the time for the round-trip to upstate New York. He had every confidence in my ability, however. I would do just fine.

And, up the Thruway in the growing dark, I did. The K75 was solid at speed. The cold of the early spring evening slipped down my neck, past the old electric vest (unconnected) that Ryan had pressed on me before I left. I was not prepared for this, in any way. I realized, as I rode on, that I knew nothing about this machine. I knew where to add gas when the time came, but beyond that, nothing. I had been too excited to get a motorcycle to educate myself about it. The idiot lights were, to me, hopelessly foolish idiot lights. I carried no tools, no spares. I did not own a cell phone, having proudly eschewed their excessiveness: in the olden days, we did just fine without them, going all sorts of places such as the ends of the earth without them.

I determined to get one as soon as I got home. It was very, very dark on the Thruway.

The headlight seemed not to work very well, either. I squinted ahead into the blackness. When I switched on the bright, the pavement below disappeared into some abyss, and the trees above became a crystalline arch. I could not slow enough to avoid outriding my headlight, because I would have been rear-ended going twenty.

And still, I was suffused with a sense of joy at this rightness. This was exactly where I was meant to be, this road, this speed, this throttle, this hymn of mechanical strength intoned by the constant engine, my companion now. It was coming back to me, rushing back to me, all the miles of all the rides of a time I was now unpacking from a dusty steamer trunk. *That's it—I remember now!*

While going straight, I was circling, riding back to the person I'd been. Thus, the overwhelming feeling of that first ride, frighteningly unaimed lights and all, was of completeness. I was whole again. All I could do was trust in this machine, that it would do what it said, by its very stalwart existence: take me home.

. . .

**ASK AND YE** shall receive, at least among motorcyclists Sharing information is a favorite pastime; receiving it is a right, as well as a rite. That is how I came to be at the Park 'n' Ride lot outside Poughkeepsie, with a sizable check already made out to the pretty blonde who stood before me. "Ride around for a little bit. Just let me watch," the instructor said. I took a few turns. Not tight ones, though that is why I came. There was a magic key, and she was going to give it to me. Then I would be restored, all would be as it used to be, and I could dispense with this cold gnawing that had become constant. I had spent weeks riding local roads, passing the sloping gravel drives of friends, wondering if I would ever feel I could turn in to them. I rode on past scenic turnouts, and sometimes a mile past a necessary U-turn, just so I could find an expanse large enough to accommodate the four lanes it seemed I required to reverse direction. Apparently, I had become the motorcycling manifestation of the country-western song titled "Give Me Forty Acres (To Turn This Rig Around)." I was fine as long as I kept going. It was stopping that made my head start hurting. If I did not consciously think, *Brake gently, stop* exactly *on center*, the front discs locked tight and the forks dove down, then up, ready to destabilize this monster of weight.

I come back and cut the engine. The first question she asks is, "Have you named your bike?" "No," I reply. "Have you figured out the gender?" "No," I say again, after thinking. "I don't think you've bonded yet with your bike," she says. Without further explanation, I understand, fully. I stare at the side of my machine and see it as if for the first time, and I see that it has been reaching out to me, in its stoic way, offering numerous opportunities to trust. I blanch inwardly as I recall half a dozen episodes when she might have dumped me but didn't (always close; it was always close), each one in its discrete clarity like a flashbulb memory, a shock. I remember each sloppy stop, each turn suddenly aborted, each too-wide reverse of direction. Now I feel a little ember start to flame into red as I stare at my bike and think: *You were trying to teach me something—and in fact you can teach me everything.*

Then the feeling stopped because I wanted to get on and ride, draw S-curves in the parking lot (missing the commuter buses occasionally pulling through). I wanted to look like the instructor, gracefully riding my bike.

She characterized my machine as one that did not particularly like to stop. Good; I felt corroborated here. BMWs don't, in general, she said, which is why they're the ones that get ridden so far. But also, she offered, there seems to be something wrong with your forks.

I could say things to her that I could not to others, and she in turn told me about how her riding had changed after she had had children. I knew her questions to me would have been scoffed at by others—naming your bike! so twee!—but they were approaching that region where intellect had no purchase. This was the place where everything that you are conjoins with the distilled sensation of moving through time and space.

To do something with competence is its own reward. It puts a sense of rightness into the air around you. Fluidity. This is the moment toward which we aim ourselves, into the dissolution of all moments. And then: timelessness.

To fall out of that grace suddenly, to hit the earth with a thud, is supremely discomfiting. When competency has fled, putting a chip, or worse, a long crack, down the middle of some priceless thin china, It is terrible.

I knew what I had to do; I just could not do it. I could not turn my head all the way around to look where I needed to go. I feared that if I did not stare right in front of me, I would find myself suddenly down. I was using the wrong charm, and I knew it.

But I went out the drive of the Park 'n' Ride an hour and a half later full of promises. To myself, and to the K75. I would beat this. I would have to. Or I wouldn't be much of a rider anymore.

• • •

I WAS a different rider now. I moved back and forth between two worlds, mommy world and motorcycle world. They had different people in them, different priorities, different codes and language.

Citizens of these separate countries couldn't understand why I didn't fully inhabit one or the other, and I could not explain. Did I want a unified life? No, I just wanted time to be endless so I could continually slip through the crack between the two people I was. I wanted all the time in the world to put on a dress and go to friends' for dinner, drinking wine on the patio and discussing the current presidential administration while the children played in the backyard. I wanted all the time in the world to go motorcycle camping and ride to Florida and talk merits of tires and spend whole days taking pieces off engines and cleaning them and putting them back.

I did not have all the time in the world. All at once, I knew. Time had become rare, elusive, choked off and breathing hard. While I was going on my way, I had unwittingly made a passage of some moment.

There is a time like a bridge—let us say it is the age of fifty. On one side of the bridge is forever: no idea of "end" intrudes on anything, especially one's daydreams. Tell the forty-somethings, then: Go, have your big parties with your big platters in your big houses. Sometime soon, it will all seem too big, too full of infinite hope; a little pointless. Life's vista has narrowed. That is when you have crossed over the bridge, and that is when you find yourself thinking alarming things: *Holy shit, I may, if I am lucky, have something like twenty-five, maybe thirty, years left. And I'm not going to be riding into my seventies, probably: some people do, but perhaps they shouldn't.* Enough said. So—fifteen years left. That means fifteen *seasons*, those ever-shorter leases on fine weather that blaze by and melt into cold.

And it hits you: You will not get to go everywhere on a motorcycle that you want to.

Motorcycling causes dreaming. Like a virus causes the flu. It makes you imagine far reaches, and long to get to them.

I rode down country roads and, as I always had, looked yearningly at all the pretty houses, in all their different styles—*there's the modernist me! and there's the Victorian! and, oh, the prairie style I always thought I'd have!*—but now disappointment followed as quickly as the punctuation at the end of a sentence: Get real. When would I have this, and that? In my other lifetime?

That is what riding now gave me. An aching longing for another lifetime. At least one, please. Then I would once more have large garden parties, and wear those gorgeous black slingbacks.

But I had given them away thirteen years ago. I could not wear such things anymore.

A strange sensation washed over my riding days now. It was the knowledge that I was riding toward the end.

. . .

ONE DAY I find myself riding through the town in which I got married, but I do not stop the bike. I don't want to look, and I feel the synesthesia of half a dozen emotions: a chill of loss, a nausea of morbidness, a heat flash of hopeful thanks.

# 5. Those monumental days

Deep, deep, and still deep and deeper must we go, if we
would find out the heart of a man; descending into which is as
descending a spiral stair in a shaft, without any end, and where
that endlessness is only concealed by the spiralness of the stair,
and the blackness of the shaft.

—HERMAN MELVILLE, *PIERRE; OR, THE AMBIGUITIES*

A story with no beginning and no end.

—INSCRIPTION ON DESERT ROCK, IRON BUTT ASSOCIATION MEMORIAL
NEAR GERLACH, NEVADA

**EVERY MARCH, FOR MANY YEARS,** members of the league of the
proud, the few, the addicted—also known as the Iron Butt
Association—shook the ice off their souls and gathered to welcome
the advent of another riding season. Even if, to most of them, the
riding season has no end, and thus no beginning to celebrate. Just
find an excuse, then.

It was held in Daytona Beach, Florida, in conjunction with the
fabled Bike Week, which saw hordes of motorcyclists trailering

their bikes from the still-frozen North to the precincts of warmth, and the first chance to twist the throttle since the onset of winter locked them into faint dreams of riding. This is one reason the event was later moved farther north, to Jacksonville, far enough from the armies of amateurs—the posers and squids and those for whom biking is less about going than about making a loud noise— to where they could be alone with their own kind. Those who quietly understood. At first it was a simple act of getting together to breathe the same air, with boxes of pizza in a motel room the centerpiece of the event. But the association, in its trajectory toward consummate professionalism and the gathering-in of any rider who shares the belief that this long-distance craziness is not crazy at all—true crazy is attempting to limit risk to the point where a sort of living death occurs—moves relentlessly away from pizza in boxes.* By 2007, there are thirty thousand members from forty-four countries; two years later and fifteen thousand more have officially joined the ranks. The rate of growth is becoming exponential, even if the nature of the endeavor, and the fact that it provokes raised eyebrows from the always vaster majority of motorcyclists, means that extreme long-distance riding will remain a fringe activity. Nonetheless, take this for example: In 1995, thirty-eight Saddle-Sores were issued, four Bun Burner Golds (fifteen hundred miles within twenty-four hours), and one 50cc (cross-country in fifty hours or less); in 2000, there were fifteen hundred SaddleSores, 250 Bun Burner Golds, and fifty 50ccs. The infection has spread later-

---

* "The fact that most *normal* motorcyclists don't find anything fun or rewarding about Iron Butt rides is part of what holds the LD community together," writes Paul Yeager in the inaugural issue (January 2010) of *Iron Butt Magazine*, in a blunt appraisal of the inside/outside split.

ally, too, to farther reaches of the world, with Turkey now home to its own branch, called the One More Mile Riders, which certified four SaddleSores in 2001 and invited Mike Kneebone, presently a world leader of sorts, to visit. An e-store now sells IBA merchandise to its members.

So the organization has come to require a hotel with banquet facilities to house its early spring gathering, and another to host its biennial summertime national meet at which seminars are presented over three days ("Battle Ready: Ride Preparation Rituals"; "Dealing with Digital Data") and which costs $250 to attend. (Wait—"3:00 p.m.: LD Riding on a Budget"?)

And thus blooms a paradox: the institutional growth of a collection of people engaged in an essentially private, individual pursuit that needs to remain largely invisible in order to survive. Now there is an ever-larger group organized around something that in its nature is opposed to organization. Ralph Waldo Emerson was the great illuminator of this modus vivendi, writing in "Self-Reliance": "Society everywhere is in conspiracy against the manhood of every one of its members. . . . The virtue in most request is conformity. Self-reliance is its aversion. It loves not realities and creators, but names and customs." The Iron Butt Association has become a society that has been quite busy of late giving names and customs to the creations of its self-reliant members. An image now may occur to the contemplative: a rope being pulled in opposite directions, finally snapping from the strain. Then the loners will have to think up some way to subvert the calcified conservatism that is the final end of all societies. The *true* outsiders will form their own hidden group. And it will begin again.

This urge, this need, will persist. It has to, because it is bigger than any flag that flies over it.* Or perhaps *bigger* is not the word. Perhaps *insidious* is.

• • •

**AT THE GATHERINGS** of this long-distance tribe—or at BMW rallies, which are somewhat the same thing, frequently tinted with endurance colors that have leached out in the wash—you see one or two people wearing T-shirts that read I ♥ ARDYS. They are insiders to the insider group, because they are celebrating one of their own, one of the really exceptional. It makes your jaw drop to hear what Ardys Kellerman, a seventy-six-year-old great-grandmother, has done. It is at once beyond belief and the usual unusual list: four Iron Butt Rallies; a 50cc; at the age of seventy-four, 80,131 miles in six months, including three SaddleSores; seven hundred thousand lifetime BMW miles. More than twenty-eight times around the earth's equator. You see her everywhere. Because she rides everywhere.

Why? Yes, well, why does DNA do what it does? A single mother of four children, she began her riding career on a small Yamaha, then graduated to a Honda CB360 before discovering BMWs, in particular the oilhead RTs trimmed for touring. She received a pilot's license, but she learned that she felt most at home on a motorcycle. Especially when she was riding far, and riding long. Now, she may be claimed by the years, the accumulation pulling her slower and slower toward the soil that will call us all home, but on a motorcycle she becomes ageless.

The halt and the lame, the graceless and the disabled, the gray and the potbellied, all see the years turn back (and back) on a motor-

---

* Long-distance rider Jim Abbott writes, "Eventually you will need to complete a 12-step program to stop this sickness (just make sure to get an acceptable receipt)."

cycle. They become the image of grace again on a bike. It may be harder to lift the leg over the saddle, but then the throttle, mediated through the powerplant, delivers immortality to the rear wheel. We fly into the perfect motion of youth. We do look handsome out there, don't we?

The median age of motorcyclists in 1985 was twenty-seven. By 2003, it had become forty-one; a quarter are older than fifty. That is why gray heads seem to predominate at so many gatherings of bikers, especially those devoted to machines that are out of reach of most except the financially secure, such as BMW (leading the company to realize that unless it somehow entices a future generation of buyers, it will soon be out of business; hence its program called Camp Gears, to encourage young riders). It may be that motorcycling can no longer compete with the new age's digital excitements. The young now prefer standing on street corners, at bars, sending texts to one another. They are living in the future, one where a promise in a message is received and returned, a future that moves further off with each successive *send*. They seem to be missing the present, the one that receives the world, streaming past, through the senses.

Or so I think, from my vantage as an old person. I do not really know anything about their world.

But I know they do not know very much about mine, either.

Bob Higdon is another who encompasses the secret of this alternate universe, the one made of miles under wheels. That total of 1.1 million miles he has ridden on BMWs means he has out-Ardysed Ardys by some fourteen circumnavigations of the globe. As a retirement gift to himself upon leaving the law—*some gift*, snort the sane—he rode a County Courthouse tour, visiting every county in the contiguous United States: 3,069 of them.

Dave McQueeney, a slight man who looks like the friendly shoe-maker in a fairy tale, with an elfin, private smile always lighting his face, his long gray ponytail rappelling down his back, is in fact a demonic presence in the long-distance world. He has conceived of some of the more extreme rides, because he long ago dispensed with the easier ones. That is a relative term, of course. He came up with the 50cc Quest, as well as the Washington, DC, thousand-miles-in-one-day. He once rode the Four Corners but required the challenge of a small twist: returning home to Los Angeles to retrieve a different bike for each leg. He has ridden through the lower 48 in ten days. He completed sixteen consecutive one-thousand-mile days. And he has accumulated 1.6 million miles (by now, more) on, you guessed it, BMWs. He says he, like all truly committed long-distance riders, does it simply to "prove to ourselves, not to others, that we can do it." When Mike Kneebone describes McQueeney's unprecedented, inexplicable accumulation of miles to an assembled crowd as "sick and twisted," he does so with a happy smile.

It is received with understanding by a fellow like Steve Branner, who finished thirty-seventh in the 2007 Iron Butt Rally. From the moment he learned he would compete, he says, "I had no control of my life for a year and a half; the Iron Butt Association controlled it." As he rode toward the end of those monumental days, the ones in which all machinery, mental and mechanical and mathematical, had to keep firing against the wishes of the clock, of the miles, to pull it back to deadly stasis, he rode into a sort of euphoria. Just finish. Just attain relief. The last ten miles, he reports, he was on himself continuously, like the minute hand, repeating silently: "Don't mess up now!" Later, he says, talking to a fellow competitor who didn't finish was like "trying to console someone after a death."

I am talking to Thomas Coppedge in the bar of a Ramada, I

think it is. Or maybe a Marriott. We are in a room filled with guys (and a few who are not), a disproportionate number wearing suspenders, with large midriffs and gray hair; the retirement years are made for piling on miles. "I ride for the ride," he tells me. "Take the opportunity to do what you want. 'I wish' is not in my vocabulary." He is a commercial fisherman, so he can't ride at all during what most motorcyclists think of as "the riding season." Instead, he does all his riding in April and May, thousands and thousands of miles, more than many will ever do in a year, or several. He did his first SaddleSore, then quickly embarked on a Bun Burner Gold, and followed them with a Great Lakes Ride, a tour of some 2,450 miles in under a hundred hours. He has ridden to Hyder, Alaska, the southernmost town in the state, seven times. "Sometimes it's beautiful, sometimes it's crummy. So what?"

A story. That is what they get. A narrative that orders life. We are the animal that created the campfire tale to make sense of the otherwise insensible.

A ride is a classic story, with its beginning, middle, and end. I suddenly see that this is the true ignition of the riding enterprise: giving smooth literary form to the incomprehensible. Bound together, then, are listener and teller, each in turn. Robert "Hoagy" Carmichael, drink in hand, tells me how he once peed in his pants after a long ride in a cold rain. His hands were so numb he only managed to get off the first five of seven layers of clothing. Couldn't do the zippers on the rest, and then. . . . The event is transformed here in the hotel lobby, from dismaying fact to Story. We are bound. Coppedge says, "The great thing about this group is that I've got friends all over the country, so when I need a place to stay, all I do is . . . ," and he mimes putting a phone to his ear.

Home is everywhere.

. . .

**WE MUST BELONG** to something. Even in our endeavors that call for us to be alone.

"We do it to prove to ourselves, not to others, that we can do it."

Richard Hillary was one of those fearless RAF pilots who appear in old movies, dashing in their flight leathers, the thin line of smoke issuing from their pipes as eloquent as any brave speech. He died in World War II. Before that, he wrote *The Last Enemy*, about the Battle of Britain. In it, he describes his decision to fly under the Severn Bridge. And he thereby describes, fully, the chivalric code of the endurance rider: Do it, say nothing, and by those two acts, say everything about a certain manner of living life.

*[Said a friend:] "Richard, from now on a lot of people are going to fly under that bridge. From a flying point of view it proves nothing: it's extremely stupid. From a personal point of view it can only be of value if you don't tell anybody about it."*

*He was right, of course.*

*To fly under the bridge now simply to come back and say that I had done so would be sheer exhibitionism. It would prove nothing. Yet I knew I would fly under it. I had to for my own satisfaction, just as many years before I had had to stand on a twenty-five-foot board above a swimming pool until I had dived off.*

So the long-distance ride becomes ever more extreme, the top of the mountain resists the planting of the flag, as we push it farther toward the clouds. The long-distance rider who excels becomes more rare, more consumed by the attempts that require him to strike out alone—and there he finds his tight community of other rare individuals. They are drawn together by a common knowledge of their suffering—the suffering that feels very much like relief.* As well as by the sweet knowledge, individually held but communally celebrated, of the triumph attained alone. (The yogis trained themselves to get by on four hours of sleep, "rising with joy from our sleep to another day's work of study and exercise," according to one Western convert in the early twentieth century.)

I find an answer to my endless questioning, this relentless worrying of the strange irony that is the togetherness of loners, in a 2009 book about the solidarity of people brought together in times of crisis. Its title speaks directly to the long-distance-riding enterprise: *A Paradise Built in Hell*. Ha-ha. There is a great difference between the unasked-for disaster and the freely undertaken adventure, of course, but the effect created in those who endure them both is the same. We were made, it seems, out of material that needs above all to persist, and never to quite feel so alive as when we try. In her account, Rebecca Solnit might as well have been writing about riders in a rally, but she is actually quoting the original codifiers of this peculiar occurrence of social unity. The first is Samuel Henry Prince, a resident of Halifax in 1917, when an enormous explosion in the harbor killed more than fifteen hundred and destroyed every building within a mile. He studied at Columbia University and wrote a dissertation in the new field of sociology on what that disaster could teach us about basic elements of our behavior. "He compares the crisis in an individual life to that of a society in a disaster," Solnit

---

* Mightn't there be some small, tenuous connection between the extremely long ride and the psychological/neurological illness of self-mortification, such as cutting, which both causes pain whose chief purpose is to deflect attention from a more insistent underlying pain *and* self-medicates, by releasing endorphins that seek to heal?

observes of his premise: "'Life becomes like molten metal. It enters a state of flux from which it must reset upon a principle, a creed, or purpose. It is shaken perhaps violently out of rut and routine.'" ("I've never been bored on a motorcycle," said Steve Branner.) A few decades later and sociology had become a credible branch of study. Another survivor of disaster could now turn his firsthand observations into scholarly ruminations on what happens to the social animal changed by fire in the crucible of war. Charles E. Fritz, an American who had served in the Army Air Corps in World War II, wrote of what really happens to us in extremis, and why:

> The widespread sharing of danger, loss, and deprivation produces an intimate, primarily group solidarity among the survivors, which overcomes social isolation, provides a channel for intimate communication and expression, and provides a major source of physical and emotional support and reassurance. . . . The "outsider" becomes an "insider," the "marginal man" a "central man."

What I see before me in the buffet line at the Marriott are men (and women), marginal in the greater world of motorcycling, who have become central in their peculiar world, long-distance motorcycling. They reach for the dinner rolls and share quietly the "intimate communication" that only "survivors" of brutally long rides are able to share. They are in the warm embrace of what their cold, lonely trials produce. And they find it good. Beautifully, and vitally, good. Fritz went on:

> People are thus able to perceive, with a clarity never before possible, a set of underlying basic values to which all people sub-

*scribe. They realize that collective action is necessary for these values to be maintained and that individual and group goals are inextricably merged. This merging of individual and societal needs provides a feeling of belonging and a sense of unity rarely achieved under normal circumstances.*

This is why they do not need each other when they ride—to be alone with the challenge and the risk, the sleep deprivation and the intense focus, forms the "disaster" that they will "survive"—but why they necessarily come together when they stop. The ensuing "group solidarity" has a name: the Iron Butt Association. And then they finish dessert while listening to a speech by the association's head. They do not know it by the sociologists' term, but they are eating the fruits of an intense human experience. It is either given to us against our will, or, when not, self-created on hellishly difficult rides. In Rebecca Solnit's book, I read what it is called: *redemptive disaster.*

# 6. *Why?*

*One who pressed forward incessantly and never rested from his labors, who grew fast and made infinite demands on life, would always find himself in a new country or wilderness, and surrounded by the raw material of life.*

—HENRY DAVID THOREAU, "WALKING"

*You do not belong in the middle. You're better off when you . . . go to extremes.*

—SAGITTARIUS HOROSCOPE, JUNE 5, 2010

**WHEN I TURNED FIFTEEN** or sixteen, my parents finally had the wherewithal to graduate from the swim-and-tennis club—clear on the truth-in-advertising front, those were the only activities it provided, other than a drinking fountain in the locker room—to the country club. This was the full upper-class American experience, circa 1929: Tudor Revival clubhouse, acres of clipped emerald grass on which to chase small white balls, clubhouse bar, immense dining rooms with white tablecloths and obsequious waitstaff, cotton balls in glass jars in the obliquely named powder room. I was encour-

aged to go to the teen dances held within this anachronistic clois-
ter, in the vast hall bookended by fireplaces that could consume a
full-grown person standing up, not to mention a timid teenage girl.
"There are such nice people there," I was assured. But I felt assured
of nothing then, except the fact that I did not belong there, or anywhere. I did not belong at the country club, and I did not belong in
any of the groups I saw arrayed before me like branches of the military, each with their own uniform, extensive training regimen, and
code of behavior: cheerleader, druggie, debating club. I wanted to
belong to something; I just did not, by virtue of something as deep
in me as my very mitochondria.

In June 2010, I did not feel I belonged to the ranks of the long-
distance rider, either, but at 5:15 a.m., the dawn of a gray day that
promised nothing but unending wet, I nonetheless walked out of the
Clarion Hotel in Northampton, Massachusetts, into a parking lot
filled with them. Then, exactly fifty-two minutes later, seated on my
new R1150R, engine idling and awaiting the slip of the clutch, I was
told by two men standing by with clipboards and stopwatches, "Go."
Three minutes earlier, the bikes lined up three abreast ahead of me
had been similarly waved out; three minutes later, the trio behind me
would leave. We were to be back no more than twenty-four hours
later. I felt like a pretend long-distance rider; I only hoped my unmask-
ing would not occur too soon, such as in the next sixty seconds, by
ending up in the bushes lining the hotel drive or taking a left into a
right-turning rider bent on a hasty start in the annual Minuteman 1K.

The plan to enter my first rally, what I hoped would be a begin-
ner-amenable initiation into the madness—*only one-eleventh the
duration of the Iron Butt Rally; simple addition, as opposed to high-
school calculus, right?*—was again launched in the calm air of too-
far-in-the-future-to-be-real. I had done my thousand-mile day. Now

I would simply add bonus-searching and picture-taking. I had had my digital camera for six years and had yet to discover how to turn on the flash. Or what other features it might be hiding behind its menu screen—I suspected many, since my son could occupy himself for hours with it, making movies and slide shows and special-effects sequences. But I was not too proud to ask a ten-year-old to instruct me in one of the essential aspects of rallying. I'd figure that out later. I was sad, for a number of disparate reasons, that one of the great American photographic media, the Polaroid, had recently gone extinct and thus passed out of rally usage. At least I knew how to take a Polaroid photo: Press the button.

The matter of the GPS was slightly more complicated; I did not own one. They were becoming increasingly necessary, and only one or two rallies out of the dozens held each year were doable without one. It did not have to be motorcycle specific—at eight or nine hundred dollars, the rainproof version was owned by only the most committed technophile or rallyer (still, lots of those), while the rest made do with plastic bags over lesser models. Several friends offered to lend me one for the weekend, so I figured I was covered. And then came the news, a couple of weeks before the rally start, that the bonus locations would be made available only by their latitudes and longitudes two nights before we were scheduled to convene in Massachusetts. My fond imagining of spending a few hours leaned over a paper map spread on the living-room floor, tracing a route between points with a highlighter, vanished as fond imaginings are wont to do. There was no way even to know where these mystery spots were located—what small byway of the millions possible between the rally's outer boundaries, inscribed by the Erie Canal on the west, the Atlantic Ocean on the east, and not ruling out another country to the north—without feeding it into mapping software. That was a bridge too far, by several rivers, for me. Yet waiting to determine a preliminary route until after the rally banquet the night before—when the bonus packets listing the locations' descriptions would be distributed—would be foolish if not impossible: riders had a meeting at five-thirty in the morning and would start to leave at exactly 6 a.m. Staying up late the night before I anticipated riding most, if not all, of the next night filled me with a cold dread. I had not pulled an all-nighter in so long that I could not even remember whether it had been for fun or for work. My body clock, after years of regimented risings in advance of my child's school-bus arrival, was set to get irredeemably sleepy by ten-thirty at night.

At bedtime on the Wednesday before Friday's trip to Northampton, I was ready to pull the plug on the computer, surrounded by all-too-breathless lists of things to remember to pack—*heated jacket! extra oil! insurance declarations form!*—when I hit Send/Receive once more. There it was: the bonus list, at last. When I opened one of the three different files in which it had been sent, a page of numerical gibberish appeared, looking quite like a chart of marine soundings. There was nothing I could do with it. There is a certain relief in giving up all pretense of control, or caring. I went upstairs to sleep.

There is a certain relief, as well, in delivering yourself to the mercy of someone who has presented himself as a savior. Enough had happened lately, in the past two years of an utterly changed life, to convince me that motorcycles and the people who ride them would always appear in the breach, just when I thought all, or most, was lost. It never was; it was to be found, but in different places, the Easter eggs of joyful fate. The latest materialization came via Facebook, something I had previously considered a fairly harmless time-waster or version of a high-school popularity contest. I had friends (or Friends) I'd never met. I knew only, from their profile pictures, that they rode motorcycles. Indeed, that was (as ever) enough to make them actual friends. But there it stayed, the occasional "Like" effortlessly hit in order to maintain the appearance of connection.

On the Minuteman forum that had leapt into life a couple of weeks before the start, a venue for questions about requirements and procedure, someone had posed a surprised query about needing a GPS; this rider protested that he had none. I was relieved—I was not alone in this world after all. I quickly wrote of my happy leagueship with the other Luddite—whereupon I was informed by rally staff that the other rider in fact did not need one, as he was registered as a SaddleSore entrant. The rally had two sections, one of which would simply be following a prescribed route to qualify for Iron Butt Association membership. I was registered to run in the rally proper, for which I had to have a GPS and the mapping software to digest the locations before they even got to the GPS.

I would not even have known there was a thing called mapping software—in much the same way that I discovered there was a device called an iPhone, on which one loaded things called "apps," which originally dumbfounded me the previous Christmas, when the California cousin I fondly refer to as the "Surfin' Priest" entertained a table of our offspring by upending it slowly as if drinking, whereupon the screen's beer-suds imagery seemed to disappear down his throat; *quelle nouveauté!*—if it weren't for the ceaseless discussions of *Streets & Trips* (versus whatever) filling the digests of the LDRider listserv. Not to mention John Ryan's kvetching that the technological transformation of rallies these days meant that endurance and riding skill were now supplanted by inputting: "It's like having Bill Gates run your rally for you," he sniffed in dismissal. At any rate, I should have known better when I learned about the Minuteman rallymaster, whose custom-appointed Iron Butt Rally bike was featured on the website of the northeast's foremost BMW dealership: it was a spaceship from the future, loaded with gee-whiz gadgetry I had last seen on Saturday-morning outings with the Jetsons. Rallies take on the personalities of their leadership. Some are rife with jokes. Others are the product of a grown-up boy's dreams of James Bond's world.

. . .

**THEN A MESSAGE**—*O magic of this far-flung universe of motorcycle friends!*—appeared in the in-box: "Hi, Melissa. I'm happy to bring my old GPS for you to use." Lovely surprise that it was, the offer was bootless without the knowledge of how to input this useless collection of numbered coordinates. Then: "And I'll load the bonuses on it before I come."

The offer came from Doug Jacobs, a fellow I'd never met. He'd previously run an Iron Butt Rally, so I'd be in the hands of someone who knew what he was doing. As I was gathering my e-mail from the computer in the lobby of the Clarion on the afternoon before the start, I saw a man with two leashed Shar-Peis watching me. "Hello, Melissa." I loathed putting pictures on Facebook, but now I was glad I had. Doug had had to pull out of the rally himself, but he came all the way from Rhode Island to deliver the GPS and my good fortune. As a favor to someone he'd never met.

Why was the world suddenly offering me these unasked-for riches—always, it seemed, by way of motorcycles?

After another anonymous hotel buffet (*I'll have the salmon, please*), we repaired to our rooms to plan routes. Only I repaired to Doug Jacobs's, because there was nothing in mine that could have helped me get anywhere. I was in way over my head. Now I hoped only that I could do something that remotely resembled finishing the rally; secretly, I hoped I was not doing something beyond inept, unto danger. Before I left home, a friend had remarked darkly, "Remember, Melissa, that you have a child." As if I did not know that, did not feel the pressing weight of that inestimable responsibility, every moment of life.

Upstairs, Doug spread out his further gifts to me: handsomely laminated maps of possible routes. He offered one plan, that of going for only ten of the highest-value bonuses and bypassing the dozens of smaller bonuses that would sap time better spent on riding to the farther-flung ones. I could decide to ride to Boston (some would), or to Long Island (some would), or to Montreal (ditto). But at this hour, when I felt I should already be feeling the hotel's white sheets against my legs, a borrowed alarm clock ticking near my head, I could not make decisions. I had to make lists.

I would take a counterclockwise tour, starting through Massachusetts, up the coast and along the edge of New Hampshire and into Maine, onto a lonely high road to bag two thousand points and then repeat the road until I could head west through the neck of the state back into the peak of New Hampshire. In Vermont, when it was dark and I was at last getting tired, the reasoning went, I would ride the unsurprising superslab south and find one more bonus, for 750 points, and head directly back to the hotel. For a little sleep, I imagined. How long could it take to ride 1,097 miles, anyway?

I transferred the requirements of the bonuses—*take a photograph of the entrance to the ski lodge*—onto paper, in some kind of numbered sequence that made sense to me, and that would include the number of the next location I would punch in on the unfamiliar GPS. I was putting myself entirely into its hands. The only guide I would have was it, and my penned list. I took a look at the laminated map, then folded it away.

As I compiled the list that was like a ladder I would climb, even as I laboriously hammered its rungs into place bad carpenter that I was, my head started to hurt in exactly the same way it did when I was trying to balance my checkbook. When I did that, I always had the impression I was at a loom, placing strands of yarn between my fingers to keep them separate. When I reached the sixth strand, and then the seventh, my stomach clenched. *If I drop these, I will have to start all over again . . .* and I couldn't. Not now. I had to sleep.

The borrowed alarm rang at 5 a.m. I retrieved the bottle of fruit juice I had put in the room's small fridge the night before, and drank while I pulled the curtain back on the incipient morning, a pink-gray promise. Oh, that was just the sodium lighting outside in the parking lot. Now I saw that drops of water flecked the window. The National Weather Service was right this time: it would rain most of the weekend. Well, why not throw that into the mix, eh?

The theme of the rally, since they all must have one, was "That's Entertainment." All the bonuses would have something to do with the rubric—sites of concerts and plays, along with a subtheme concerning the Grateful Dead. They appeared everywhere, apparently. From the first turn out of the parking lot shortly after 6 a.m., with adrenaline surging through me and fuel through the 1150R, I fled toward the Ogunquit Playhouse, where I was to count the number of flagpoles. This had to be a trick question. There were ten. So there had to be another, somewhere. But there wasn't. "This rally rewards reading comprehension." I stood there and recounted, then wrote *10* uncertainly in my bonus book. I recorded the odometer reading and then remounted for another hundred and fifty miles of riding. My mind, my world, was reduced to only the road, and the imagining of what the next waypoint would look like. I never succeeded, instead finding places that in their true specificity would stay with me long into a future where the postulations had long vanished. I rode by the log-cabin Rockwood Chapel in Maine three times, circling in increasing frustration the area the GPS's little checkered flag told me was here; it was not. Or not exactly. And exactitude was what I needed, dammit. I was not going to quit on this one, having ridden fifty miles up one of the most secluded roads in America—the long hour of which I spent running through possible scenarios of what would happen when I ran out of gas, which seemed imminent—to get two thousand points. This sucked my energy as surely as the climb in elevation was draining the fuel in the tank. (And why was it that I hadn't just tootled around Vermont instead, taking a leisurely tour of the Green Mountain State, then stepping into any store to purchase a bottle of Vermont maple syrup, which, when presented with the receipt proving it was bought in the state of origin, would have yielded a gigantic bonus pot of three thousand points? *Why?* After having long given up on the type of nine-to-five gift shop I reckoned would sell such a thing—alongside flat circles of chocolate candy cutely named Moose Droppings and mass-produced "hand-loomed" sofa throws—at the last fuel stop in the small hours of the night, I watched a BMW rider emerge from the twenty-four-hour convenience store. He was fairly leaping. Above his head in triumph he lofted a plastic container. "Maple syrup!" he cried to the night air. Of course. This was Vermont. They sold maple syrup next to the Advil and the engine oil.)

Another three bonuses, another three photos of a towel bearing a large black *48*. It was taking too long to dismount and remove the towel from my bag, my camera from its pocket, the booklet and pen from its plastic bag, then reverse the process. Why had I not come up with a system for this?

Why had I not known how beautiful central Maine was? And

how full of moose? Oh, and construction, whole sections of road torn away to reveal rocky mud underneath, which I rode in first gear with my tongue between my teeth. Cars followed within inches of my rear wheel; their drivers inexplicably were not thinking intently, as I was, of what would happen if I slewed sideways and slipped to the ground. The impact would not hurt me much, but their wheels driving over my bones certainly would. I tapped the rear brake to flash a warning: Back off, *please*.

By the eighth of my goals—Lakeside Theater in downtown (and simultaneously uptown) Rangeley, Maine—evening was nigh. By the ninth, an empty lodge at a desolate-seeming ski area, nighttime had descended (preceded by a blinding downpour that settled my remaining question about how rainproof my left boot was). Before, it had felt lonely. Now it felt lonely and strange, riding through a world where people had vanished, but not the sad, empty shells of their domiciles left dimly behind in the dark. I could trust in nothing anymore but the yellow line on the small screen that showed through the plastic bag Doug had taped over the GPS. At least I was about to hit the interstate and the promise of *south*, south and ultimately sleep. It was two-thirty in the morning. The GPS directed me to the on-ramp, and on I went. The next sign I saw read MONTREAL, 68 MILES. You could not have slapped me across the face and caused a more stunned hopelessness. I was too tired to argue with a digital device. I had simply erased the fact that the tenth bonus was north, because I did not want it to be. I wanted this to be over. Enough with the fun.

One more photograph in the dark, down a soggy sand path toward the Franklin County State Fairgrounds, a few miles south of Vermont's border with Canada. I parked my bike and almost didn't care if it fell over. I had thought I would be done hours before this.

There were 190 miles before I reached the Clarion Hotel—which I was beginning to think of as the Abode of the Blessed. I was beyond counting, or remembering. Then, suddenly, I was beyond being awake. I recognized this feeling, and it frightened me. It was the feeling right before I nodded off. I sang, loudly. I opened the face shield, to feel the last stinging drops of cold mist. I stood up on the pegs. I shook my head. And then my front wheel hit something, a bump, and I woke. That is how I knew I had fallen asleep. At 75 mph.

*Remember, Melissa, that you have a child.*

This was absurd, coming this close to leaving him motherless. For what? For a lark. "Just to know I can do it." I should stop. Have a nap.

But I knew myself, and knew that if I fell asleep, it might be hours till I woke. And then I would be time-barred. What I had just spent the past twenty hours doing, the lonely miles of the past twenty worried hours, would be for nothing. I could not throw it away now.

I headed for the first lighted sign off the highway, the big white, blue, red CHEVRON looming over the darkness of trees a promise. Ah, so this, *this* was why I had foregone my very necessary morning coffee for the past two weeks, enduring the afternoon headache that signaled withdrawal. For the Styrofoam cup that now was my hope.

Back on the road, I congratulated myself. There! You are awake again!

Until an hour later, 4:30 a.m., when the feeling was coming over me like a shroud again. Well, if it worked once, then it would work again, wouldn't it? It was all I had, in my thinking that had gone all wrong. *I can get back by 5:30. I can finish, and I can sleep.* So, Putney: another cup. I was a few miles from the last bonus, and I did not care. I was not going.

Two BMW riders pulled up in succession, filled their tanks, then spun out of the station in the direction of the last bonus. Energetic young men. I stood by the pump, draining my paper cup.

I do not remember how, but then, at last, I was near. I had tapped in the last location: Clarion Hotel. The GPS showed me the way. And that is how I came to be on a dead-end street of quiet houses where families, parents and children, still slept the sleep of unknowing. The light gradually spread upward from the edges of the world. I backed the bike, rolled forward, and rode on, disregarding the screen. I think I know where to go now.

I pulled in to the hotel's lot an hour before the final window closed. Volunteers with clipboards checked my mileage on the odometer. I parked, but sleep—not yet, again. There was still scoring to do, where I would learn what terrible mistakes I had made that would get some hard-won bonus disqualified. But after sitting at a long table beside others who likewise sat in front of volunteers who held their futures in their hands—in the form of the digital cards they had taken from our cameras to put into readers plugged into laptops—and likewise silently prayed their reading comprehension had not let them down, I learned mine had not. All ten of my bonuses were allowed. My syrup was impounded (to reappear in the large vat of heated syrup next to the pancakes at the breakfast buffet and awards ceremony). At last, at long last, I dragged myself to an upholstered bench in the lobby. I put my sweatshirt over my head. Now, when it could, no sleep came. Members of a girls' sports team, greeting the early morning and each other jubilantly, and loudly, passed to and fro, flip-flops snapping against their bare feet. From the close dark I was breathing underneath my head cover, I wished them dire harm. Then it was time for breakfast. I rose.

. . .

**A WEEK LATER,** I look backward to where I think I was, and it seems it was a dream world: one made solely of night, and drive, and the motorcycle I'm on. That is all there is.

. . .

**BEFORE,** I had been telling a friend about the structure of the rally, how it is conducted. The expectations, and the seriousness with which it is taken. "But this is *so* not you," he exclaimed. "This precision, these calculations. It's a military exercise." I am a bad soldier.

. . .

**IN MARCH,** four months earlier, I had spent hours chipping a layer of ice from my driveway with the blade of a shovel to clear a narrow path so I could leave for Jacksonville, Florida, and the annual Bike Week meeting of the Iron Butt clan. It would be the last big ride I would take on the K75. I had a new electric jacket liner and gloves, and a heavyweight balaclava to wear under the helmet. I had a new rear tire. And I had the highway.

Once on it, I think about how I am both inside and outside. But neither, fully. If I were simply a literary observer of this gathering of the tribe, it wouldn't be such a point of pride to ride a bike there. And for what? Four days on the slab, passing by places where I'd dearly love to stop—Savannah! So near this place my father had taken me once, in a long-ago childhood where the history of the South had filled my dreams, and my scrapbook—and only two days at my destination. Cutting six days from the child-care calendar was a difficult enough slice. *What am I, a writer or a rider?* I was all mixed up. For ten years I have been regularly mishearing the question, "How's your writing going?" "You mean my riding?" Sometimes it *is* "How's your riding?" and I think they're asking about the writing I'm not doing.

Alone, I rode through a wet snow outside of Washington, DC. Accompanied by the sight of the Blue Ridge Mountains, running parallel to the interstate I was on, I remembered the incomparable pace of the road that ran along their crest, and the slow dance for which it held out its hand. Now, on I-95, my brain split in two another way.

There is nothing I'd rather be doing: riding feels good (at least until it feels bad, which it was shortly to do, with dark and wet and cold conspiring together). But at the same time, I realize this ride is nothing short of loony: straight-line highway for a thousand miles. To go have dinner with a bunch of people for whom this is normal behavior. Then to turn around and come home.

I actually feel sorry for my rear tire. I want it to be well rounded, as it were, having lots of varied experiences. Instead, it is flattening in the middle, mile after mile after mile.

It is amazing how draining are the cold, the rain, the traffic, the speed, the dark: all trying to beat you up. (And indeed, in the morning, in the hotel mirror I will see the flesh under my eyes hanging alarmingly in arcs.) At the last gas stop before Jacksonville, I suddenly discover I've lost my coordination. It's a startling moment. I grab a handful of brake all at once, which causes the K75 to lurch to the right, the side on which it always wants to go down. At the gas pump, I can't aim the bike properly and almost go down again. I am cold to my core. I have been eating out of gas-station convenience stores for two days. This has felt long. And not entirely happy, even if I am happier now on a bike than anywhere on earth.

Near the end, though, I pass by a long line of evenly placed sodium streetlights. Suddenly, to my left, a shadow biker passes me swiftly, then another, and another, every three seconds a shadow of myself going too fast disappears ahead of me before another races up from behind. There are dozens of them, all perfect, all me.

· · ·

**WHAT DRAWS YOU ON.** On the return from Florida, I ride northward into another season, the cold one again. I was seriously tired, and shivering, even with the control set high on both jacket and gloves. But strangely, the farther I went, the less thought I had for stopping. Like every rider with a privately held goal, I had somewhere I wanted to be: home.

Something was pulling me, strongly, through the last ninety miles, late and dark. It was cheese and crackers. I could taste the Triscuit breaking apart in my mouth, the creamy resistance of some Camembert against my tongue. Cheese and crackers have never been so thoroughly dissected—existentially, philosophically, chemically. Cheese and crackers, followed by a hot bath. I could feel that, too. I would sink in up to my neck, the vapor warming the air up to my hairline. That is all I thought about, all I felt.

And then I am turning in to the driveway. Sidestand down. Lights spilled from the kitchen: he was there. I pulled off the helmet as I walked, peeled off the balaclava. The door opened. My boyfriend walked out toward me, holding a plate. "I thought you might want some cheese and crackers," he said.

· · ·

**I AM NOT** like them. I look at them, and think of them, and consider them, what they are doing on their persistent long, hard rides made of not stopping. But when I ride by the enticing billboard, the historical marker, the restaurant serving hot meals over a long hour, I become myself: the curious, the slow. I want to lie on my back in the warm grass and watch the clouds moving in their inexorable unmindfulness.

At a highway rest area, maybe southern Ohio, maybe Indiana or Illinois, who knows, my riding partner and I sit in the shade by the bikes, eating dried fruit and nuts and drinking lots of water against the day's pressing heat. A Honda Gold Wing turns in and parks next to our machines. He is done up head to toe in Aerostich, the mark of the serious long-distance rider. She, behind him, wears a matching modular helmet. That way, they do not have to unbuckle in order to drink, or eat. It saves seconds. Our gear is strewn on the grass beside us.

We talk, of course. They are heading to Hyder, Alaska, and back. From Florida. In two weeks. They met six weeks earlier, he says, referring to her as his fiancée. That is how I come to think of them as Jack Sprat and his wife, for she is as round as he is lean.

Two weeks—for somewhere around 7,400 miles? This means they will have to keep a pace of 525-mile days, every day. They will become intimately acquainted with every rest area and gas station, but not much else, along a route that will certainly be slab all the way. This they referred to as their vacation.

The man has done this kind of riding for a long time; it is the only kind of riding he does. He has read all the books related to Iron Butt rides, but he has never documented his own; he has never bothered with the membership card. Again and again, members of the IBA told me they were brought into the official fold only because they chanced to see the license-plate back of someone who was a member; they were already long-distance riders without knowing it. I wonder how many unofficial Iron Butt riders there are. (Probably a whole starry universe of them, gathering in the ether of the Motorcycle Tourer's Forum, where ride after ride—"I'm thinking of Mexico in April—who's in?"—is posted and shared and photographed. These are not group rides, with clots of bikes backing up traffic, however. Some rides are listed as "Long Distance," meaning *we're going, and not stopping,* others as "Flower Sniffin'," which simply point to a spot on the map at which to meet and light out on day rides, and still others as "Power Sniffin'," which is described as "flower sniffin' on fast-forward." Then they convene in the evenings to do what motorcyclists do best—ride the ride again, in the imagination. That way, it can be enjoyed twice. There are countless wandering nomads in the far-flung tribe, each of whose primary address is "on the bike.") The rarity—Bob Higdon says that, with the proportion of LD riders to the six million motorcyclists in this country, "You're in the dim netherworld of 1% to 2% where access to full-time psychiatric care should be a matter of human right"—is less rare than I thought.

As they leave (their rest stop has taken place in half the time of ours; we are still sitting there heat-stunned when the Gold Wing departs), I wonder about the peculiar drive pulsing inside that sort of person. No wonder they got engaged so quickly; he found one of the few women in America who met his prime qualification: one who wants only to ride.

I had noted a curious sticker on the back of both their helmets, advertising a website. When I got home and brought it up on-screen, I gasped audibly before quickly X-ing it away. Pornography of the most graphic type imaginable; the sort that makes my sort of person blanch. There are so many strange drives encompassed by the human animal. Some even make extreme long-distance riding appear modest.

• • •

**IF INDEED** long-distance riding is the latter-day expression of our evolution as forest-dwelling survivors of a tense daily life-or-death battle, it is perfectly natural. It is also aberrant, taken to extremes. It becomes a monomania, the sun so hot at its center that it burns down everything else. "Anyone who excels at a singular pursuit must become somewhat one-dimensional," a long-distance rider says. They have an unusual amount of time in which to reflect on what they do.

In a 2005 study on monomania in literature, the scholar Marina van Zuylen unwittingly writes about the central emotional component of what pulls the long-distance rider onward, and it is not cheese and crackers.

> *The idée fixe is an infinite source of comfort; not only does it provide unshakable boundaries, but it lures the subject into a sense of agency.*

*Agency*: "the capacity, condition, or state of acting or of exerting power" (*Webster's 11th*). "Boundaries." In other words, attaining "comfort" . . . through *dis*comfort. Aha. Paradox, again. It always comes down to that, our primal endeavors. In order to survive, we destroy. The monomania is "a lethal attachment to a discipline that promises to put complexity on hold."

I think about something Doug Jacobs had written about his experience running the Iron Butt Rally: It was, in the end, absolutely "simple."

And, it seems to me, simply damned heroic. Or maybe it just looks that way, to an outsider.

# Pause

## MOTORCYCLISTS ENDURE

Britons Kevin Sanders and his wife, Julia, hold the record for
riding the seventeen thousand miles from Alaska to Tierra
del Fuego, thirty-five days, in 2003. The *Wall Street Journal*,
in a January 8, 2010, article on an Argentinean motorcyclist,
Ivan Pisarenko, who had spent four years traveling the route,
reported: "The number of people . . . attempting to ride the
length of the Americas has grown at least tenfold in the past
decade, to roughly 2,000 a year." Despite the fact that this
figure must certainly be greatly inflated, it is also true that
"adventure riding," of which long-distance riding is a large sub-
set, has been growing as a sport: sales of touring bikes more
than doubled between 1998 and 2008. The outsider activity is
now extremely popular.

There were eighty-six sanctioned special rides listed in late
2010 on the Iron Butt Association's website, including such
small matters as the Transanatolia (West to East Turkey in
less than twenty-four hours; three completions); Circuit of Ireland (a lap of the country in less than a day; four finishers);
Gibraltar to Nordkapp in three days (seven certificates); a
SaddleSore 7000 (a week of thousand-mile days; four completions); Black Sea to the White Sea in thirty-six hours (one); the
Why? Whynot! Insanity (Why, Arizona, to Whynot, Mississippi,

in twenty-four hours; one finisher); and the South Africa Four Corners Ride Gold (none—so far). New rides are being added all the time, as the association magnetizes riders from all over the world, with branches in Taiwan, Russia, Finland, and Ireland. Among others. To submit a ride idea, you just need to have a concept that is, in President Kneebone's words, "interesting and twisted—preferably both," and to map it. Oh, and ride it first.

.

Simon and Monika Newbound, of Great Britain, left from Dublin in 2002 with the goal of breaking the Guinness World Records achievement of a continuous ride of 99,600 kilometers (61,900 miles). In three years and one day, they completed their round-the-world trip (which included fifty-four countries and every state and province in Canada and the United States), on their BMWs (F650GS and R1150GS). Their ride was formally recognized by Guinness in 2005 and listed at 183,000 kilometers, or 113,700 miles.

.

Two Canadians, brothers Colin and Ryan Pyle, set a Guinness World Record for their 2010 motorcycle journey around China, the "Longest Journey by Motorcycle in a Single Country." They spent sixty-five days on the road circling China on BMW F800GS bikes. Their 17,674 km journey was the first by riders who fully circumnavigated China by motorcycle in a single journey.

.

Don Arthur, retired surgeon general of the U.S. Navy, in 2002 ran the Motorcycle Tourer's Forum Four Corners tour (Maine to

Key West to San Ysidro to Washington) in four days, ten hours, and forty-two minutes—the fastest time ever.

•

In 2001, Phil Mattson cranked out thirty consecutive Saddle-Sores (a total of 30,603 miles) on a Harley FLHTCI to master the IBA's self-styled Longest Month ride. In May 2003, Michael LaDue did the same, on a Honda GL1800.

•

Bob Hall won the 2001 Iron Butt Rally after opting to go from Sunnyside, Washington, to Madison, Alabama, the very long way: via Prudhoe Bay, Alaska. (One thousand of those seventy-five hundred miles were on unpaved roads.) This route netted him a million bonus points. Two others who attempted to get these points were time-barred at the final checkpoint.

•

Team Strange Airheads sponsored an "I've Been Everywhere" tour in 2000, based on Geoff Mack's country-western hit that recites place names at a frantic pace (Reno, Chicago, Winslow, La Paloma, Charleston, Houston, Springfield, and so on)—ninety-two of them. Two hundred people entered. Only Dave McQueeney visited every one of them in the five months allotted.

•

In 1995, Gary Eagan of Salt Lake City rode 1,932 miles in twenty-four hours. He did so with no auxiliary fuel supply.

•

Gary Orr rode coast-to-coast nonstop, 2,232 miles, without ever putting a foot down—from San Diego to Madison, Florida—using a trailer hauling gas for his BMW K1200LT. A

November 2008 *Rider* magazine squib on the feat was titled
"Depends?"

·

John Ryan's fastest certified SaddleSore, of the countless
thousand-mile days he has completed, is thirteen hours and
forty-five minutes. He accomplished it at 2009's Redwing 19,
a Virginia charity ride established to benefit children who had
lost parents in a Special Ops debacle in Afghanistan. Ryan
came in first in a field of more than five hundred.

·

Lisa Landry, rallymaster and events coordinator of the Iron
Butt Association, rode her Gold Wing, as the organization
truthfully says, a "staggering" 3,146 miles in less than forty-
eight hours, on the invitation-only Cognoscente Group's soi-
disant Blister. (Mike Kneebone of the IBA says, "If I were asked
to identify a quality that separates us from other motorcyclists, it would be self-discipline." Apparently.)

·

The most "self-disciplined" of them all may well be Wisconsin
state senator Dave Zien, who in July 2004 reportedly rode a
1991 Harley for thirty-one consecutive thousand-mile days. It
was a long Longest Month, as the IBA terms its ride of thirty
consecutive SaddleSores, July being one of those months with
an extra day. As if testing self-discipline for a "short" month
were not bad enough.

# 7. A difficult road

*I love him who makes his virtue his addiction and his catastro-*
*phe: for his virtue's sake he wants to live on and live no longer.*

—FRIEDRICH NIETZSCHE, *THUS SPAKE ZARATHUSTRA*

*I do not call you Far Rider because of your great races and fine*
*pony, but because you are one who rides far from himself, and*
*wishes not to look home.*

—*HIDALGO*, 2004 (SCRIPT BY JOHN FUSCO)

**ON THE NIGHT OF MAY 19, 1927,** Charles Lindbergh went to a
hotel near Roosevelt Field on Long Island, hoping for two and a half
hours of sleep before taking off in the *Spirit of St. Louis.* He had
every confidence in his plane's design, which he had overseen, and
its nine-cylinder Wright Whirlwind engine, but he also knew that
six people had died previously trying to take the Orteig Prize, the
$25,000 award for the first nonstop transatlantic flight. Perhaps that
knowledge contributed to his inability to sleep at all. And so he took
off—laboriously, for his plane was carrying 450 gallons of fuel—on
a 33-and-a-half-hour flight without having slept in the previous

twenty-four hours. An unsubstantiated report says he had conditioned himself to stay up that long by once going without sleep for forty hours; now he would be pressed to the limit, trying to stay awake for fifty-five hours.

He had stripped down the *Spirit of St. Louis* to its essence: what would get him up, and over, and there. People thought his attempt was suicidal. He would fly with no radio, in order to save weight. He had what they call a "feel" for flying, including a preternatural mechanical understanding of his plane. The wicker seat was uncomfortable, which Lindbergh had considered a benefit, as it would aid in keeping him awake. He also had requested that the plane be made unstable, so that if he took his hand off the stick or the rudder, the craft would dive or turn. He once said, "What kind of man would live where there is no danger?"

On his flight, when the sun rose over the ocean, the persistent fog had at last become patchy, and through it Lindbergh saw "numerous shorelines," with "trees perfectly outlined against the horizon." Since he knew he was still in the middle of the Atlantic, where he was skimming only feet above the water, he realized that these had to be mirages. He was hallucinating from the exhaustion, from the desire to arrive at land.

Later, the *Aircraft Yearbook* would note that his performance was undertaken without publicity, "like a job that was to be done, whether the world knew of it or not." The pilot said, "I was attracted to aviation by its adventure, not its safety, by the love of wind and height and wings."

Lindbergh did not seek fame, though it came to find him. He was shy, a loner, and these were the qualities that ultimately suited him for what he accomplished. He was not prepared for the reception. Mainly, he wanted only to test himself and the machine he flew.

• • •

**CHARLES LINDBERGH** bought himself a cup (for fifty dollars, a large sum then) that condensed breath into drinkable liquid, so that he could save the weight of extra water on his flight. Was it any more ridiculous—as some laughed incredulously—that eighty years later John Charles Ryan should wear an external catheter to shave three minutes per restroom break during his own quest to establish an endurance record?

Perhaps not, if one tallies the host of uncanny similarities between the two: both inward, boyish, handsome, politically conservative, humble, residents of moneyed precincts of rural New Jersey; both would claim that their achievements were largely due to others.* Both eschewed tobacco and alcohol, remained leery of the press, insisted on being self-sufficient and alone, were generally indifferent to food, and possessed excellent manners. They disdained small talk and were deliberate in answering questions. Both proved to be accomplished and engaging writers (Lindbergh won a Pulitzer). They shared grace and skill with their respective machines, which enabled both to live through youths filled with daredevilry that might have killed those of lesser natural gifts.

Yet what Ryan accomplished was celebrated only within the small circle of motorcyclists who knew that he had done it. As is the custom among members of the Iron Butt Association, the applause was restrained, although he did receive a rare show of admiration in the form of a standing ovation nine months later in Jacksonville.

---

* In Jean Renoir's impossibly perfect film *La Règle du Jeu* (*Rules of the Game*), made twelve years after Lindbergh's flight, the character styled after the famous pilot and named André Jurieux lands from a twenty-three-hour Atlantic crossing and explains modestly, "It's the plane's doing."

Ryan was destined never to become as widely known as Lindbergh, of course, though for a time he was recognized wherever he appeared with his FJR. He was not prepared for the reception.

• • •

**CHRIS SAKALA** could be considered one of the very toughest of the World's Toughest Motorcycle Riders. He has competed in three Iron Butt rallies, placing second in 2005 and fourth in 2009 (his BMW GS Adventure quit the 2007 rally well before its rider wanted to). In 2003, he decided to go after the record for one of the most extreme rides the Iron Butt Association recognizes, the Ultimate Coast to Coast. It asks a rider to ride between the southernmost point in the United States and the northernmost: Key West, Florida, to Prudhoe Bay, Alaska, above the Arctic Circle, a distance of more than fifty-six hundred miles. It asks a rider to do it on some of the worst roadways in North America, in the most variable weather, but it does give the rider some latitude in choosing the speed at which to attack: the IBA will certify a UCC completed within thirty days. That makes it a difficult ride. The way Sakala and Ryan approached it was to push the difficult toward the lonely reaches of tolerance.

Through sheer will and drive—the Dalton Highway is a highway in name only, being 414 miles, some of steep grade, along largely unpaved road built for maintenance of the Alaskan oil pipeline, with only three towns (of under a hundred total population) along its length—Sakala beat the previous record of 126 hours by coming in at 114 hours and forty-nine minutes. As he approached the Alaskan endpoint of that ride, after traveling what he called "the road from hell," Sakala would later write, "I was ready to be done. I was at the limits of my riding."

Five years later, John Ryan would complete the ride in 101 hours, taking more than thirteen hours off Sakala's record but still over the ninety-six hours that had been posted in 2004 by Gary Eagan, on a Ducati. For some reason this stuck like a burr under his tail, and Ryan was irritated into another attempt. He wanted to drive a new record so far into the ground that no one could ever pull it out. All the stars and planets in the universe would have to align just right—the weather, his blood-sugar levels, the FJR's mechanics, a formidable amount of money with no appreciable sponsorship, U.S. border guards in a relatively good mood, the assistance of dozens of people—and Ryan would wrench them around with his bare hands if necessary. He knew that the window opened and closed quickly in the first week of June. His starting point would be Deadhorse, Alaska. But first, he had to ride there. Ryan only ever rode; the only time a bike of his would be lashed to a trailer would be when it could no longer run, or its rider was scheduled for surgery, or, more probably, both at the same time.

On many Iron Butt rides, including the rally itself and the basic SaddleSore and the Bun Burner, slow and steady wins the race (even though they are technically not races at all). Indeed, the first-place finishers of the rally in 2003, 2005, 2007, and 2009 did so at an overall average of 45–48 mph. Breaking legal speed limits is either openly discouraged by the organization—and if done will remain unpublished in its official recognitions—or is not done simply because it hinders the success of the endeavor. Excessive speed is fatiguing, and it wastes fuel, making for more frequent stops, which is where time is lost ("Keep the wheels turning" is rule number one of endurance riding). But there are no rules, and no laws, in the sphere of extreme record-setting. Every type of achievement that breaks boundaries also breaks laws. Those who will be remembered forever for their jaw-dropping feats—like Philippe Petit, who walked a tightrope between the twin towers of the World Trade Center in 1974 with dazzling disregard for all types of laws, including gravity's—always seem to celebrate their finish by getting hauled away by the gendarmerie.

Before this type of celebration could be hoped for, however, the ride had to progress past the status of budget sheet. The benefit lunch in New Jersey had filled the coffers only partway. Four days before his scheduled departure—the window was starting to creak closed—there was still a considerable shortfall. Letters and phone calls to Yamaha for further assistance, beyond several spare parts they already had provided, went largely unheeded. (Many of Ryan's supporters were incredulous that the company did not see him as a PR plum dropped into their lap. In the midst of a recession that was hitting the motorcycle industry hard, he would have made the perfect poster boy for a campaign that could have recast the FJR as the Energizer Bunny of bikes.) Then, at the last moment, a lone star in a nearby galaxy whirled into place. Someone with imagination employed by the Metzeler tire company saw the potential that could be realized with the donation of just a few sets of tires. They were shipped to prearranged locations along the route. Ryan finished his packing.

So that the troubles could have a chance to begin. Just before leaving home for the ride west, he discovered a cracked wheel rim that needed to be replaced. On May 27, he arrived in Fairbanks, where he got new tires, repaired a zipper in his Roadcrafter suit, and worked to fix his malfunctioning CB radio. Then, twice, he was turned back by icy roads on steep grades in Atigun Pass in the Brooks Range on the North Slope. A dual-sport rider from Alaska, Jack Gustafson, who accompanied him partway on a Kawasaki KLR 650, could not make it any farther than Ryan did on his street machine. The FJR got a flat tire. On June 3, at midnight, when his original schedule had him racing somewhere along the interstates of Minnesota, in the middle of his ride, he phoned to say that a rock had punched a hole in his oil pan. He hadn't made it to his start yet. He was still twenty-six miles south of Prudhoe Bay, close enough to catch a whiff of arctic sea.

It is a good thing that in the oil fields of the Far North, expert welders are not hard to find. They made him a new bash plate and stoppered the hole with J-B Weld and a sheet of aluminum.

On May 29, "AKBeemer" (Kevin Huddy of Fairbanks) had posted a message to the BMW Motorcycle Owners of America (BMW-MOA) forum, reporting that Ryan was on his way up the Dalton Highway with Gustafson. The plan, once he got to the starting point in the tiny village of Deadhorse, was to turn around and, after the clock started, make Fairbanks in seven to nine hours (after 498 miles of gooey, or possibly snowy and gooey, track; Google Maps estimates the time, presumably in a carefully driven car with a functioning heater, as nearly twenty hours). There, he would go to a car wash, spray off the amassed mud from his wheels and radiator, and reinstall his hard bags, being held there by Huddy and his wife, Annie.

On May 30, though, Ryan was back in Fairbanks, unable to get through the snowy pass in the Brooks mountains without traction. On May 31, he started north to Deadhorse again but turned around once more with a flat tire; he was back at the Huddys' in Fairbanks. On June 2, he replaced his rear tire and had a bracket for his windscreen repaired at a local fabricating shop. On June 3, he turned north again, and that is when the rock sliced the oil pan; he continued upward, but this time under tow. On the phone he sounded dispirited—but only in the Ryan fashion, which was to be dejected when prevented from riding, not in fear that he wouldn't—and grateful for the help he was receiving, the balm for all motorcyclists' hurts. He could now simply hope to start his run on Friday night, June 6.

Bob Higdon writes of the Haul Road: "It's a difficult road in a difficult and unforgiving part of the world. And it breaks things—first your bike, then your heart."

For the next thirty-six hours, there was only silence—no phone calls, little news on the online forums. What was happening up there? Ryan no doubt was in what one might call his fight head, one hundred percent on task. Nothing existed but his hard eye sighting down the barrel of the weapon he was fixing to fire. (How rare in life; how few will ever experience anything remotely like this obliterating focus. I wonder if it is calming or bracing; both, I hazard a guess.)

The absence of news increased the desire for it. By links and e-mails, the audience at home was growing, eager for whatever dispatches would be posted by anyone online. They read, while sitting in warm, dry dens, AKBeemer's next report: "His resolve to do this has not faltered even a little."

Then, at 12:55 a.m. on June 1, he starts to "do this."

Every masterwork begins with a single small stroke, and for any that is intended to be recognized by the Iron Butt Association, it is the same one: the acquisition of a time-stamped receipt. Ryan's bears the imprint of a Tesoro gas pump in Prudhoe Bay. In addition, he was required to have a witness form; it was signed by several people from Brooks Range Supply, a tool-and-machine-parts shop open twenty-four hours a day, 365 days a year. The production of oil is too valuable to ever cease, and the machine parts provided by this shop ensure that it never will. There is a perfect symmetry in a consummate act of fuel-burning beginning where the fuel is first brought forth.

Nine hours after he first opens the throttle, John Ryan is south of Fairbanks. He is, at last, doing what he was improbably created to do: *cranking*. He is, at last, alone with his machine and an exceedingly long road. Where he most desires to be. His thoughts circle around the only things there are for him now: what is in his immediate vision—a new view every microsecond—and the complex mental calculator that runs constantly, adding, multiplying, dividing the numbers that will mount quickly into miles. He likes being alone with these thoughts moving like rushing water. Over the first twelve hours, he averages 70 mph—in the strange perpetual daylight, in the rain, in the mud. He completes 1,678 miles, a long Bun Burner Gold, in twenty-one hours. And on he goes. We know this for what it is: impossible. In our collective disbelief, we stay up into the night facing our glowing screens; the e-mails that fly back and forth are all we have to reconnect ourselves to reality. Otherwise, we could only imagine this small fleck flying through the cold dark, and we would become as unhinged as he seems to be. Higdon hits Send: "I don't know how to describe this ride so far, and trust me: I've seen some prodigious turns of the screw in my day."

A select few have been given the password to access Ryan's SPOT Satellite Tracker page, where his progress across half a continent is visible from transmissions that arrive in twenty-minute increments. It becomes obsessive, watching an animated dot inexorably moving across the large map; the emotions fill in the gap, and the image of a lone human, battling time and miles, simultaneously crosses the screen and the mind. It is obsessive, but then so is this ride. Unto anxiety, at least in the watcher. I cannot turn off the power. My heart races.

The way it makes me feel, sitting at home in the cushion of indoor heat and cushioned chair, to be receiving these transmissions of his progress through what I imagine to be a dark and frozen land, is what I think a member of a nineteenth-century whaling captain's family must have felt, receiving letters from a watery world so far away it was impossible to conceive.

Then, on the third day, he apparently stops—for nearly five hours—outside Eau Claire, Wisconsin. No one knows why. Only questions come into my in-box; the answers are now sickening guesses. The password to the SPOT tracker page has gotten out, and so many try checking it all at once that it freezes solid. Now the BMWMOA forum is the only source of updates, most assiduously desired. People are verbally agog. The thread winds onward for eleven pages; there is another on the ADVRider forum, and even one on the New England Moto Guzzi list. At last, Ryan starts moving again, or at least the transmissions from the tracking unit do. We won't find out until later that he had simply forgotten to reset the SPOT unit; he has in fact been moving all the time. He is streaking toward his goal. The Metzeler PR man's girlfriend, a pilot and photographer, is also infected, and she decides to get into her plane and fly to Key West: the end is assured now, in sight. After riding through anything, nothing could stop him now.

(Although, toward the end of that first week of June 2009, John Ryan had indeed been stopped, briefly, by a law-enforcement officer in Illinois; he had been riding thuddingly hard for two and a half days with only a few hours of sleep. This did not include the previous tense week of false starts due to weather and mechanical plagues he had endured just attempting to start the ride that to this point had taken him about four thousand miles. He got off the bike and removed his helmet. The trooper, startled, asked if he was all right. He apparently did not look as though he was. "Yeah. You?" Ryan replied. He was trying to hide his annoyance, because [at least at that particular moment] there was no probable cause for a stop. The officer had not been around to witness the speeds Ryan had been achieving during a twelve-hundred-mile stretch of continuous rain so frustrating to the rider that he drove the speed up and up in a perverse attempt to spin the rear wheel; that large number will remain officially unpublished by any organization, including this one. Ryan explained to the cop where he was coming from, where he was going to, and why. Then he asked, politely, if the officer would run his license as quickly as possible, because this was costing him time. When the trooper returned his card, he told the rider to be careful, and wished him luck. "Thanks. Careful and lucky are the only way to get this done." Indeed.)

On the BMWMOA forum, someone brings up the inevitable Safety Question. Just as inevitably, others jump on him.

"Why hasn't anyone else on this thread questioned whether or not this is a safe activity? . . . Do you want to be on the same highway as someone who has ridden 5,000+ miles in 96 hours?"

"If it's John Ryan, I do," replied another. "I just wouldn't expect to keep up with him." It's signed, "Jim, who's ridden with John a lot of miles. A lot."

Someone else chimes in: "I'd take it over some BDC* in a minivan yelling at the kids or talking on a cell phone." Case closed.

Key West, the southernmost point in the United States, reached by a two-lane road over a hundred miles of archipelago, can be a stubborn traffic knot impossible to untie. But you need brakes to do that, and Ryan's front pads had already been used up, in less than half their normal life. Right after he reached the end, he would have to pull those calipers, and the Alaska mud that still occluded them. These are the thoughts he was having as he threaded his way to the

---

* Brain-dead cager.

end, not the possibility that anyone was waiting for him. The idea was too eccentric to occur to him. Or at least it was until he stopped at a gas station, and the attendant came out holding a phone, asking if he was John Ryan? A well-wisher in Minnesota who had been following on the SPOT page had searched for Ryan's whereabouts on Google Earth and was phoning with congratulations. It was Ryan's first clue, surreally Big Brother–ish, that what had previously felt supremely alone had in fact been shared. He asked the caller how he had found him. "Thousands of people are following you online," he was told, to his incredulity. It was only to become more strange when he finally pulled up in front of the yellow-and-red buoy that marked the end of the journey. There, a woman with a camera, and others, crowded around him. He had figured he would be there by himself, as he always is at the end of a ride, and at the beginning, and in the middle.

He did not seek fame, but it had found him.

· · ·

**THE LONGEST** seasonal migration of any oceangoing mammal is that of the humpback whale, some four thousand miles. It is a glorious mystery.

The forums were ablaze.

"Massive achievement."

"Unbelievable. What a ride."

"The SPOT page is killing me!" (Response: "Probably takes longer to load a page than it takes him to drive across a Key.")

"An incredible feat."

"GO JOHN GO!!"

"This is more impressive than an Iron Man Triathlon."

"Simply amazing."

"What a feat of determination and endurance."

"What an event in motorcycling history!"

. . .

HISTORY CAN BE fickle, lionizing some (Lindbergh), forgetting oth-ers. But before that will come into play, we pause to genuflect before the statistics: long-distance endurance riding belongs to statistics, as miles belong to it. Rides are endlessly sliced into ribbons—length-wise, widthwise—until they are rendered into long streams of per-centages. Numbers amaze.

65 mph average overall. 72 mph moving average, after sleep is factored in (2 to 2.5 hours per twenty-four-hour period). 5,645 miles. 5,191 minutes. 86 hours, 31 minutes. Smashing the previous record with the hammer of 9.5 hours. Numbers amaze.

Someone took it upon himself to superimpose Ryan's route over a global satellite photo of North America, tagged, "Now this should put this ride in some perspective . . . ," which it did: a signifi-cant chunk of the planet seen at once, traversed by a long, long red line. Two days after finishing this feat, he is describing the annual day of parking-lot rides he and his Skylands BMW Riders club members give at New Jersey's Matheny Medical and Educational Center for disabled children as "the highlight of my riding year."

He did not immediately fall into bed and sleep at the Key West home that was opened to him by a motorcycling friend; instead, he got out his phone and began calling everyone who had contributed something, anything, to making the ride possible. It took hours to thank them all.

Still, for a few days more, the discussions continued online. On the ADVRider forum, some questioned whether it was possible to complete such a ride without the help of artificial stimulants. Ryan's response was to take a drug test. But, in typical style for him, it was not just "a drug test." It was certified *"through law enforcement, and two independent labs."*

Others carped that they didn't understand this kind of riding, and therefore it was not "real" riding, which they believed meant enjoying the landscape through which they rode. Ryan kept his fist behind his back, striking with some measured words instead:

> *I've done thousand-mile days in the twisties, without ever look-ing at speed, or the odometer. I've stopped and smelled every-thing from flowers to horseshit along the way. I've taken touring bikes on group dualsport rides with singletrack, whoops, and mud. I've done super extreme rides like the one I've just finished. I've loved them all.*

A photographer-filmmaker friend of mine has an idea that Ryan would make an excellent subject for a documentary. He takes a ride on the back of the FJR one day. On his return, I see that something has occurred: "Do you always feel this way on a bike, or was it just me? Suddenly this feeling came over me, like *everything was going to be all right.*"

· · ·

**ONE NIGHT** at dinner, my son announces, "I want to lead a really epic life." I am secretly proud of such a statement: what nine-year-old thinks like this? Only a nine-year-old who may in fact grow up to do so—*my* child. And I am secretly afraid, since I also think: like John Ryan, you mean.

He has, because he is unable to avoid it, been thinking about the next ride he wishes to attempt. Forward motion defines both his enterprise and his mode of being in the world. Every step into the future is a question about the unknown. How long would it take, say, to ride from Prudhoe Bay to Tierra del Fuego? Or how about this— how many Bun Burner Golds could be stacked back-to-back? Ten? Twelve? Fourteen—twenty-one thousand miles in two solid weeks of riding . . . ? When I hear this, a numbing fear spreads inside me: *Is this humanly possible?* At some point, John Ryan is going to attempt to breach the wall between the possible and the impossible—because it does exist out there, solid, at the place where mechanics and physical endurance can finally be pushed forward no more.

I ask a friend of his, no slouch himself as the winner of an Iron Butt Rally, whether such a string of Bun Burner Golds is possible, or whether Ryan is insane to think of it. Or courting death. "It *is* possible," he says after a moment's thought. "But all of this is Russian roulette. Play long enough and there will be a bullet in one of the chambers." Ryan knows it is there. He hears it whispering, *Find me*, and he has a better chance than most of doing just that before it finds him. But.

Calculations are one thing on paper. They are always another on two wheels, at speed. It's a good place for a bullet to hide.

# 8. A family bound

We Bokonists believe that humanity is organized into teams,
teams that do God's Will without ever discovering what they are
doing. Such a team is called a karass. . . . "If you find your life
tangled up with somebody else's life for no very logical reasons,"
writes Bokonon, "that person may be a member of your karass."

—KURT VONNEGUT JR., *CAT'S CRADLE*

Open my heart and you will see
Graved inside of it, "Italy."

—ROBERT BROWNING, *DE GUSTIBUS*

**I RODE THE K75** along the handsome roads of the Catskills, into the
forested hills, and waved every time a motorcyclist passed. Every
other weekend, on the schedule of a legal agreement, I became a
single person again. I stopped for lunch in picturesque Phoenicia,
where each Sunday the streets were lined with bikes of all descriptions. I sat alone at a table and watched the groups of other motorcyclists sit down too, eat their pizzas, then gear up to depart, laughing
and talking. I went home.

Somehow, I forget now how *(from small things, large things grow)*, I learned of a vintage-bike ride that was to depart Woodstock on an early summer Sunday. The K75 almost qualified as vintage, I figured, although it was the most modern machine I had ever had. The scene as I turned in at the appointed meeting spot was a banquet for the starved: nearly a hundred bikes of all types—many, though not all, resurrected from the glory days of the forties, fifties, sixties. I was newly, suddenly, in the mood to talk; starved for it, in fact.

Before we set out in a long, slow-moving stream to lunch in another spot, someone (I forget who, though I wish I knew now, to properly fill in the historical account) informed me of a local dinner group that met every Tuesday. Miraculously, Tuesday was the one weekday evening free from parenthood that had been picked out of a hat and then set down on a notarized document while I sat in a lawyer's office looking out the floor-to-ceiling windows as tears coursed down my cheeks. I was not in a lawyer's office, I had realized in that moment: I was in a funeral parlor for marriages.

The next week, I parked my BMW outside the Chinese buffet. I went in, and there they were: my people.

• • •

**THE OLDER** one gets, the more obstinate the grip on the past. It was returning to me as I returned to one of its happiest pastimes, moments both just as I remembered them and slightly tilted by the years on sunken foundations; appropriately, riding motorcycles now caused a sort of double vision. It felt much the same—the same joy, and the same challenges. Occasionally, very occasionally, the same fears. But I felt different, and I *was* different: if eleven years—

during which so much had happened, been born, or died—had failed to mark me, then what had been hard during that time had been lived through for nothing. I had won the dings and scrapes, and they were now part of me; at the same time, I hated that I was no longer smooth and unlined and full of boundless hopes for a future pleasingly unmapped. For miles without end.

This was a new world, to be sure—one in which there were now such things as the *International Journal of Motorcycle Studies* ("From the Pleasures of the Motorcycle to the Bleakness of the Treadmill: The Dual Face of Social Acceleration"; "Hierarchies of Meaning and Value in the Classic British Bike Scene")—but it was an old one, too, in which summer weekends existed solely for the rally's call to strap the tent onto the back of the bike and go. A couple of weeks after the vintage ride, I phoned a fellow K rider I'd met there and asked if he wanted to go to Heath, Massachusetts, for a BMW rally. There was an ulterior motive, too: it was a combined gathering with New England Moto Guzzi riders. A desire, one that was starting to feel like a need, to simply look on these machines again was resurging. As we neared the rally grounds, I began to feel the fluttery anticipation of a second date. There they were!

A neat line of Guzzis old and new posed in front of a large tent over a series of picnic tables where cases of wine and offerings of food were heaped. Grills were being readied, new arrivals greeted. I stood just outside and watched: this was a family bound together by something tight and primal, something like blood. All at once I felt a pain inside; or no, it was joy and longing intermixed, the same feeling that rises into my throat when I hear those plaintive songs of Aaron Copland. It is a yearning for a place called home, that place at once permanent and pervaded by the possibility of loss.

A few faces I vaguely recognized from what I was beginning to think of as my First Life, the one where motorcycles were central to all I thought and did, before I heedlessly banished them. Still, they had come homing back to me. Or I to them. Whatever—it did not matter now. The K was parked in a corner of the field back there. I had gotten barely a nod from the Beemer folk raising their tents or gathering around the eternal coffee urn; but now, here under the banner that read, MOTO GUZZI: A WORLD OF FRIENDS, I was being embraced by people I did not know. They believed, as I felt suddenly, that I belonged with them. And with the V-twins of such mysterious power that they can create nations. My allegiance had only slept. Now it awoke.

. . .

I STARTED to haunt the Moto Guzzi listserv, an ongoing conversation among friends. Who's riding where, when; *Help—something's leaking!* This is where I saw that nothing really had changed, only the mode of delivery. In my computer was a crystalline window onto the subject of factions, and how the decision to throw in your lot with one over any other amounted to nothing less than a fully worked existential philosophy. The Guzzisti, as always, were self-aware, incisive observers of the worlds that whirled around in different solar systems. They were also funny as hell; one day I realized with a clarity of my own that motorcyclists in general were some of the wittiest people on the face of the planet. And that humor is a paramount display of intelligence.

In response to a bike-for-sale listing, headed, "Anyone need a Guzzi real bad?" John Chicoine deadpanned, "Everyone needs a Guzzi bad. Sadly most don't realize it." He also wrote that the best GPS he'd found was his "natural inability to navigate"—"It's called Get Profoundly Sidetracked."

One member who signs himself "Bird" wrote: "I was hoping someone would illuminate how I may use the Guzzi to find a wife." Whereupon another member replied, "You have a Guzzi. What do you need a wife for?"

Then a thread was started by Sean Ryder, when he posted the first "Oil Leak Haiku":

> *Drip from bell housing,*
> *Oil should be in [the] engine*
> *Instead of the floor*

"Guzzi people aren't like others," replied Bud Clauer to someone who expressed a desire to go to a joint breakfast meeting but worried he might not be welcome because he had neither Guzzi nor BMW. "I know this so well that I will speak for all Guzzisti when I say you are welcome to sit with us . . . bike or no and any brand. It makes no difference."

That was it—there was no difference. Except when there was. I was beginning to see that the cold war between Harley riders and the rest of the motorcycle world had in the past twenty years become fully armed. Now the grenades had pins, and powder. The stickers were bold—emending the specious claim that loud pipes save lives with endless variations: "Loud pipes scare little kids"; "Loud pipes lose rights"; "Loud pipes suck"; and finally, "Loud pipes, little penis"*—and so were the cartoons. *South Park* had an episode

---

* One rider has painted his sidecovers with the legend "Loud Wheels Save Lives."

that took direct aim at the antisocial noisemongers (or, as they had it, "assholes") whose narcissism masked a fear of not being manly enough. As the "Harley Problem" disrupted daily life with increasingly outrageous thoughtlessness, the *South Park* schoolkids started calling the men with their big bikes "fags." And that brought them, sniveling, to their knees.

It is not just a difference in machinery—Jeffrey from Cochituate wrote that his former Harley was "the Lincoln Logs of motorcycles" when compared to the more complex Guzzi—it is a difference in worldview. Or, possibly, a different approach to mileage. The BMW coterie that takes such pride in *riding*, in accepting the limitless offering of the road's mile after mile, sniffs at those they feel do not ride so much as pose as riders. Thus, equal disdain is meted out to Rolex Riders, for whom a motorcycle is a fashion accessory, and to those who think thirty miles—or the distance to the next tavern—is a decent day's trip.*

Now, in my second life as a motorcyclist, I find the schism widening too between the diehard BMW aficionado and those whose tastes are more catholic. The latter's scorn seems suddenly more vocal, as evidenced by one poster to the LDRider listserv:

---

* I think I may have finally, at long last, formulated at least one highly elusive distinction between Moto Guzzi lovers and those who favor the new-generation BMWs, the popular models disparagingly called "XSes" by an outspoken proponent of the "characterful" Italian products from Mandello: no one "farkles" a Guzzi. The idea is almost dizzyingly absurd. If you want a bike that you can park to attract a crowd to appreciate the latest gadgetry that can be hooked to the battery, you would choose a different bike. On the other hand, BMW attracts the farkle-happy like Tiffany's attracts trust-funders. That is why another acerbic wit in the Italian camp, Doug Ritchie, says the initials stand for Bavarian Money Wasters. And another thing I just realized. There are no posers among Guzzi riders, not a one. I hereby issue a challenge: If a reader can locate one for me, I will personally refund the cost of this book.

*I'm convinced the evangelical Bimmerphreaks were white shirt/
tie wearing, bike riding, door to door Mormons in a prior life. (No
offense meant in the least to the white shirt/tie wearing, bike riding, door to door Morons.)*
    *I find it remarkably difficult to tell the two apart.*


Those who walk the Moto Guzzi (or pre-GS Beemer) path
through life seem to have done a good bit of thinking about what
they have chosen, or what has chosen them. After one event, a
philosopher of machinery posted his reaction to the Moto Guzzi
listserv:


*In the parking lot there were but my Airhead and one other. The
rest were the farkled and techno-festooned new Beemers of every
ilk. The effect on me is the same as being in a parking lot flooded
with Harley Evo's. Glazed and bored.*


He identified the source of the boredom as the new generation of
machinery's apparent inability to elicit the call-and-response song
that defined the relationship between the rider and motorcycle of
years ago. Or, as he reminds us, the sensual nature of all physical
input and output, which becomes emotional thereby:


*The new bikes, doing everything perfectly, [require] you to learn
nothing of the bike other than to hold [down the button] after
turning the key. . . . It's a different world and relationship than I
have with my bikes.*
    *. . . We are told by faceless engineers and bureaucrats what we
need and what we are going to like. Ever seen any hundred thousand mile sportbikes?* [Well, yes: two, both owned by John Ryan.]

*. . . My very first ride on a Guzzi was a friend's V11 Sport and I will never forget it . . . I grow "horns" just sitting on one and blipping the throttle. The V11 brings out the "runs with scissors" evaluation on my behavior.*

This was what I felt awakening in me, after my eleven-year sleep: the desire to *feel* again. All that sensation—a throwing of one-self *into* (a pile of leaves, game of tennis, pillow fight)—is an animal expression of exuberance. And exuberance is the lifeblood of child-hood, the time we first understand and collect sensation. To be exuberant, to ride, is to return to the best part of life; not to remember, but to re-live.

Riding, in its physicality, connected me back with life, which itself is essentially and only physical—the body in space, the body feeling things. Thus it connected me to my mortality, because at some point I would no longer be able to ride.

As if seen through a train window at speed, desire was to me now a smear of all that I saw going by: human contact, love, the touch of another, joy, the tenuous balance between the equal grat-itudes of independence and dependence, the resolute belief that I must take what is offered and want no more, or else all would be taken from me. Riding, alone (and riding alone), would have to fill the bottomless need for connection to the world and its finitude. *The road is laid gently on top of the skin of the land, and when you ride on it so lightly—a bike provides the most minimal of contacts: any less and you'd be sitting on your butt on asphalt; any more and you'd be in a cage—you take the cloth from the skin.*

I started to feel it lift. Yes.

• • •

**I WAKE** on the morning of Thursday, September 17, 2009, to find that a spontaneous uprising has occurred. The portal through which I watch, heart near stopping, is the New England Moto Guzzi list. The first thing I see is a long thread called "V65 Lario for Melissa." If not for that word—*Lario*—I would have assumed it was some different Melissa they were talking about. It was not. They had seen a bike for sale, just like the one that I had idiotically, wrongly, let go. And now the replies were pouring in: "I'm in for $100"; "Put me down for $100 too." "I just love it when a plan comes together," John Chicoine writes in, his glee audible on the silent screen. There is some kind of infection going around; more and more chip in as the day goes by, cash as well as mechanical assistance, legwork, transportation. The thread has been renamed, to capture the act's clandestine nature and propulsive force; now it's being called "Operation Lario." One day later, John writes again: "Congratulations, Melissa—you now have a Guzzi!"

I can't move. The tears had started falling the evening before, when I had learned this was not a joke, as I had at first thought it could only be. Now I sat bowed before the computer, sobs rolling through me. These folks were simply happy—"Guzzi people rock!"— and here I was feeling something I had never felt before; I could not name what it was. I had lived this long, and I did not know what was moving through me in such great waves. It was because it was everything ever made: every joy, every regret, every hope.

Who ever gave a vague acquaintance a motorcycle? When your wife or your son gave you a motorcycle, it was an extraordinary act of supreme love, and recognized as such. But I could not fathom this. I could not fathom the strangers who together would become the beloved who thought to give a true gift: the one desired but never asked for.

"This is big. This is very, very big," I said tearfully to my mother on the phone. I could not speak of this to anyone now without utterly dissolving. I had not stopped crying for three days. "But why? I don't know!" I was searching and could not find it, no matter how closely I looked. So I did the only thing you can do when there is nothing else, and when there is everything. I went for a ride. I went to the place where the answer is always knocked free from the clots that hold it bound and inscrutable. I went to the road.

Up ahead of me then, there it was. I rode through it and, as I always do, heard it speaking as a clear, simple voice outside of me. The voice of truth.

*They did it for these things: To show you are not alone. And that love is possible.*

Now I could see it sparkling with the clarity of a thousand facets reflecting light. I realized a multiplicity of things all at once, a smallness that grew large. The love these people have for this particular machine allows them to use it to express love toward others. They do it in their everyday generosity, freely offering fellowship, and assistance, and parts. And they do it in their shattering acts of kindness. I sense they are righting something that went wrong in the universe. *Yeah, that Pierson was on a BMW!* No, not that: that I no longer believed in love. They wanted to prove me wrong.

Of course, they did not really know I needed to learn it; but somehow, too, they did. Without knowing, they knew. And they provided, with one clean gift, a silver motorcycle that looks strange in my garage even now, as unreal as youth regained, or life returning after a death, the two things I lacked in order to go on.

Inside the new Lario is a piece of the old one: a carburetor slide. Knowing it is there is both eerie (an organ from the departed!) and a comfort, in the way that something that is right feels so perfect: the weight of your child's head resting on your shoulder, the warmth of a friend's hand in your own, the surety of sleep descending like a soft, slow blanket after a day walking in the quiet woods.

People always used to ask what drew me to these bikes.

I must have been drawn to them so long ago because I knew that, at some point, exactly this would happen.

Nothing in my life made me believe in the possibility of an all-seeing, all-knowing deity but motorcycling. And I am an intellectual atheist. I just am not an emotional one now.

. . .

EIGHT YEARS AGO, someone left the world. Someone I loved like my child. When my beloved border collie died, I struggled for a way to mark this heavy, momentous passing. Something permanent. Something that hurt.

All of a sudden, it came to me: a tattoo. Her name, around my right wrist, touching the path of the blood that flowed from my heart.

Three years ago, I thought I would do the same thing: engrave the meaning of the end of my marriage on my skin. This was certainly a large event, changing everything as it had. But I never could think of a word, or a symbol.

That was obviously not the time, but this was. It was the occasion that called for the needle, for the permanence of ink under skin that would die only when I did. Now there was no searching for the right words, for they were given to me. See them there, written over my heart: *Moto Guzzi*.

# 9. More and more detached

*People are frustrated when delayed, they become depressed
when stopped. Slowing down signifies getting older, sicker,
weaker.*

　　　　　—STEPHEN KERN, *THE CULTURE OF TIME AND SPACE, 1880–1918*

*In vain I wished to find
The end and middle of space;
Under I know not what eye of fire
I sense my wing giving way. . . .*

　　　　　—CHARLES BAUDELAIRE, "THE LAMENTS OF AN ICARUS"

**WE ARE SITTING** in the Tennessee heat as hundreds of people, hands
covering their wallets as if they were six-guns in the Wild West,
stream by the vendor tents at the 2009 BMWMOA international
rally. I have never seen a motorcycle gathering as large as this; on
the grass hill beyond the concrete of the fairgrounds, tents coat the
ground for acres. John Ryan has parked the FJR on display outside
the MotoLights booth, one of his relatively few sponsors. His bike
does not want for lights.

I am wanting for a movie camera to record the various faces of astonishment as they get a load of the bike, the Frankenstein monster. Double takes, disbelief, the standing and staring and finally, finally, out dribble a few words of impressed speculation. Out come the cameras. A few people challenge, asking whether it's safe to ride like that, four or five hundred miles between stops, thousands of miles at a clip. He tells me that if he's in a mood, he'll reply: "Well, it's a lot safer than carrying that extra thirty pounds around your gut." But he doesn't; he holds his punches, unless it's a brief riposte on one of his online forums, which will occur at that safe distance that practically invites the terse goad. (To his Tuesday night riders group, Citibeemers, he responds to the question, "Anyone going to the Ear Inn tonite?" with "Not me, the socialists took all my toll and gas money"—leaving no room for extended discussion of the fact that the socialists have in fact provided all the roads and bridges that permit him to ride in the first place.)

Here is where he shows himself to be the antithesis of the precious biker, the one who cleans and polishes and accessorizes. His GPS is black-taped. Wires dangle. The fairing is scraped and punched and still bears the splatter of Alaskan mud. A thoughtful onlooker observes, "His vocation is putting a whole new stress on tires."

He is not a precious eater, either; he is not a precious anything. "He is the John Wayne of bikers," says a friend of mine. (He has "grace" and "aplomb," say two others; few who meet him do not come up with an amazement of a label. "Otherworldly," says yet a third.) His bike is conveyance and restaurant both: he eats out of his Givi topcase, avoiding any expense beyond necessary gas and oil, polishing off four yogurts in a row that were filched from the breakfast bar of the Holiday Inn Express, a lodging "too fine for the likes of me," he says. Later he will consume the contents of a six-ounce pouch of salmon. With his fingers.

Is there a pathology of directness? Of plowing through? Going straight through to the end, no matter how far, how difficult, how painful—for others, I mean. If so, I have found exhibit number one. He does not start reading a book unless he has time to finish it in one sitting (thus creating a new category: endurance reader). His approach to urban riding is that of the guerrilla, or perhaps analogous to the five-second rule for food dropped on the floor: a light that's already gone from yellow to red is passable as long as it's done quickly. He is contemptuous of anyone who doesn't ride, questioning friends, "Did you ride today? Each day you neglect to ride is equal to smoking a pack of cigarettes." His relentless drive to get people on bikes (where they belong), to place motorcycles at the very center of their lives, is not only an emblem of his persistence—which does work, if I may speak from personal experience—but possibly provides additional justification for his own choices. Or perhaps this is not a choice; perhaps it is a compulsion he is helpless to resist. One can do worse, far worse, in the compulsion arena than motorcycles. Besides, he would not see it that way at all: bikes are their own justification for an undying infatuation with them.

In his approach to women, too, one can see how thoroughgoingly formidable is his drive; as with everything, it appears to be that of Sherman on his march to the sea: leave nothing standing, nothing unburned.*

---

* Yet even the immediately apprehendable has its subterranean waters, hidden depths that both wish to be found, and to remain hidden. You know them by their low, almost inaudible sound. Outside the hotel, pack up the bike, preparing for the long journey home, alone. He is going to stay on, as always, to the very end. To the disappearance of every last soul. But he watches, nonetheless, and you suddenly see that he is torn: he wants to stay, he

The blue eyes turned on you heat a hole through your being. Go with him anywhere, and women whisper in your ear (if you are a woman, and if they assume you are "with" him), What a hunk! Oh, my! But in effect he's not real. He's a comic-book action hero. Superman. ("Get a *real* man," a true friend will advise.) He, like them, is easily readable at a distance.

These judgments—about the whole scene, the beginning and ending of the story, in a few-second glance—are given by people who, about any other person, might say, "Oh, I dunno—he *seems* nice." No, in the presence of John Ryan, the entire depth appears apprehendable immediately.

At a party, one woman who has met him only a few minutes earlier suddenly gets him in an armlock while other partygoers look on, stunned: especially her sad-sack husband, standing frozen in a portrait of misery not five feet away. In the next moment, she has climbed him like a ladder (she is short; he is not) and pressed her lips against his. For the rest of the evening, he talks to a curly-haired blonde who keeps her back to the assembled guests as if to announce, *None of you exist. Only he.* This is the one—a woman he had known years before; now she has appeared in a new guise of possibility—he stays with until late. At an Italian bike meet, he remarks that the women are better looking at BMW events, but the contrast he's really remarking on is afforded by one woman, there with her nine- and eleven-year-old daughters and her husband. His eyes rove up and down her body with the same efficiency that he processes information from the road while making time.

---

wants to go. "Don't you ever, uh, want some simple *human* contact?" he suddenly says, and that single question contains all of human history's longing, its biological, artistic, tragic yearning to join and persist and joyfully transcend. Or maybe it just means sex after all.

He indeed cannot help but make time. A male friend sends an appraisal after the MOA Rally:

*John is the perfect guy that women dream of. He nearly made me wish I was a girl. He is like a giant baby of war, a cherub wielding a sword. Soft features, baby-blue eyes, a kind voice, a cute ass, and yet he is a giant ready to protect and do battle; the perfect bad boy with all of the right things about bad boys and none of the wrong. Even if I was having a good day and feeling like I had my game on I wouldn't want to hang around with him. I'd be invisible to all women and be broken-hearted at my failure to have a personality. You can't compete with what that guy's got. I might have to kill him.*

No, one can't compete. That is the point.

• • •

**WE ALL WANT** to feel like a someone in our particular worlds (the office, the shop, the high school, the barroom dartboard), and Ryan was becoming a celebrity in the motorcycle world. It was the only world that had real meaning for him, anyway. ("I was nothing of significance before I became a motorcyclist almost 30 years and 780,000 miles ago," he wrote to a friend on a social networking site. "I just didn't know it.") But applause does not pay the bills. Ryan now seemed almost paralyzed into inaction; he seemed unable to come up with any ideas for generating cash. Although there was no one so pinnacled in the world of business that he would not phone them at home—provided he could find the number—he lacked a plan to offer them. For all his frequently stunning insight into the complexities of human nature, not to mention kinetics, he did not get the rather simple notion that all the talent in the world still needs the addition of $2.50 to procure a ride on the subway. He did not get that he could not sit back and wait for someone to ring his doorbell and hand him a bucket of money. Anyone who knew Ryan for any length of time got the unsettling feeling that he was in many ways like a large child—guileless, utterly without sophistication, except in his thinking about a certain variety of items. While he cannot, or does not, do what most adults consider basic—have a family, a career, or even a job—he can do other things most people could not do on a bet, or even under threat: ride a motorcycle brutally, brutally far. And get to where he pointed that bike.

Yet in order to raise money for the next ride—for *any* next ride—Ryan had to look farther afield. He can ignore his credit cards, but he cannot ignore the Rockies of gas, tires, and maintenance expenses that rise up, high and craggy and dark, before him. The FJR was beginning to look haggard inside, where it really counts. He needed corporate-level help. Although it was impossible that such a thing would happen, that is when it did. An apparent fixer emerges on the horizon, one who promises not thousands but suddenly millions.

A ride done for the cameras, and for charity, onto which companies will hitch themselves in peculiarly modern financial cynicism: people will buy their stuff more readily if they know the maker of the goods has contributed to a "good cause," as it makes them feel better about serving themselves without having to do anything as low as come into contact with true need. I believe they call this a "win-win" situation. For a brief moment, the juggernaut seems ready to take Ryan all the way to the Big Time.

The whole thing unfolds like a sci-fi tale, where things grow huge in the night. The infinitesimal seed from which the meetings—

replete with pie-chart presentations and file folders bursting with multipaged budgets and projected targets—emerged was a moment at a party in a downtown loft a year earlier, after the New York bike show. A moment where a writer asked, "Say, has anyone ever profiled you for a magazine? It might be a good idea," and left it at that.

There is, as they say these days, a giant disconnect between what Ryan does—the singular venture, one man and his machine moving fast along a line on a map—and what is presented for the consumption of millions via advertising and social networking, where it is transformed in the way of the soup with too many cooks. Perhaps he would re-create the UCC ride for the cameras? Of course, he would have to do it more slowly; no trying to spin the wheel late at night on a rain-slicked road; no trying to beat the clock.

But then, what would it be? A ride that I could do? A ride that you could do, and write your blog post for the five family members who would be interested in your impressions of Alaska?

In that case, it would not be a ride by John Ryan, force of nature. It would be the cadaver of what he does, blood drained from it and replaced by chemical fluids. He has always done what he wants, going with the wind; or maybe he is the wind himself, a chicane that rises up who knows when or why. He does not take direction from anyone; he makes it for himself. Literally. One evening, he is due at my house for a visit. I wake the next morning, wondering what happened that he never arrived. Descending the stairs, I pass the guest room and stop, startled, pulling my robe suddenly tighter around me. He did in fact arrive at my house, where he's never been, at 2 a.m. He soundlessly put his bike in my garage, came inside while I, a light sleeper, slept upstairs. He found the daybed, closed the curtains, and six hours later that is where I see him, asleep in his Aerostich, taking up the whole bed, hands in pockets.

He is self-sufficient, supremely so. And now he is taking in meetings.

. . .

**WHEN WE FIRST** close our eyes to sleep, the brain waves that during wakefulness appear as a pandemonium of scribbles settle down to a neat, moderately fast pattern—alpha waves. Then come the four stages of non-REM sleep: five minutes of Stage 1, in which theta waves occur at four to seven cycles per second; Stage 2 is ten to twenty-five minutes of transitional sleep in which occasional quick bursts of brain activity are mixed with calmness and poised-to-wake moments that create K-complex jolts in the waves; Stages 3 and 4 are deep sleep, which show as deep, spaced delta waves. This is where the pituitary gland releases a drop of growth hormone. It triggers tissue growth and muscle repair, which the body requires on a regular basis.

According to *The Harvard Medical School Guide to a Good Night's Sleep,* by Lawrence Epstein, MD, "When a sleep-deprived person finally gets some sleep, he or she passes quickly through the lighter sleep stages into the deeper stages and spends a greater proportion there, suggesting that slow-wave sleep is the restorative portion of sleep you need to feel refreshed." This is how an endurance athlete can go for long hours without sleep, lie down for a forty-five-minute nap, and wake up feeling adequately restored to continue: they are sleeping as efficiently as they have come to use their bodies while awake. It is a matter of conditioning acting in concert with the brain's own propensity to get what it needs under the conditions it has been given.

The homeostatic drive—the need for sleep—intensifies the longer past usual you stay awake (presuming you have a "usual"), to the point where for most of us it will be positively screaming by the time we go to bed truly late. Ideally, circadian and homeostatic drives are in concert; sometimes they are in opposition. That is when it hurts. That is when you are riding through the night. Unless you are one of the tiny fraction—less than 5 percent—who can function on four hours of sleep a night. I have a hunch John Ryan is rare in this regard, too.

For the rest of us, as one study found, going without sleep for twenty-four hours can have the same effect on the body as imbibing to a blood alcohol content of .10—DWI level.

Two things can happen when you're this tired: "automatic behavior," where you're awake and continuing to do whatever it is you're doing, but without responding appropriately to changes in the environment; or falling into microsleeps that last anywhere from three seconds to ten or fifteen seconds. I experienced the first when I was riding south through black-dark Vermont on I-89 at 3 a.m. for the Minuteman 1K. All of my depleted energy was concentrated on staying awake. If the video-arcade game speeding by my stationary motorcycle offered up a box spring lying in my lane, or a moose taking a walk, or any of a hundred options from the list of oh-holy-crap surprises that can and do appear on the road, I was in trouble. Very deep trouble. I was aware enough to know that I was flying on a wing and a prayer (or an R1150R), and that I should not be doing what I was doing. I automatically continued.

A little later, I experienced the second.

Pushing on past twenty-four hours of sleeplessness, paranoia and hallucinations can occur. Seven to ten days without sleep (as an exceedingly cruel experiment on puppies showed) can result in death.

New Jersey passed the nation's first law that criminalized driving while drowsy.

. . .

John Ryan possesses an unusually high pain threshold, attested to on at least one occasion, when he cracked open his skull in a basketball game. He discovered that he could push his finger into a place above his eyebrow where no finger was meant to go; there was the curious sound of broken bone crunching behind it. Nonetheless (of course), he rode his motorcycle home after finishing the game. Only when he began vomiting blood did he decide that a trip to the hospital was in order. There, the ER doctor advised Tylenol: it was not possible that someone who presented as Ryan did could have anything more serious than a bruise. But his sister, a well-regarded nurse, insisted that her brother be seen by another doctor, who discovered the worst shattering of a frontal sinus cavity he had ever seen, one that required a plate and thirty-one titanium screws placed during twelve-hour reconstructive surgery. Ryan was back on his bike in two weeks, after the staples closing the incision were removed and the swelling subsided enough so he could wear a helmet.

According to medical experts, such an ability to withstand discomfort and pain can be created by three things: culture, upbringing, and environmental conditions. Being raised in a Catholic household, it might be argued, accounts for all three. The cingulate cortex, the brain's "signal center," can actually choose, because of how it was wired during its development under pressure from these three factors, not to send a signal to the more primitive part of the brain that houses the fear response, the amygdala. It can instead sift through the information—I am cold; I am hungry; I am tired; this is dangerous—and basically say, Maybe so, but carry on.

In other words, willpower is attained.

It is assisted by conditioning, another element required by both the body and the mind of the endurance athlete. (A neophyte rider credited Ryan with giving him invaluable advice before he attempted his first SaddleSore: "The more extreme the ride, the more perfectly sane, clear, and logical the process of thought and action must be in order to finish the ride safely." His advice to anyone wanting to go further and attempt the Iron Butt Rally: "Sell your car. Ride everywhere.") When stress—including heat stress, or even mental stress—rises slowly, all proteins and cells in the body will produce a substance called chaperone proteins, which bind to normal proteins to keep cells from "unfolding" due to shock. They are created in response to extreme heat, cold, hunger, and sleep deprivation—all of which will occur on an endurance ride.

Well-conditioned athletes have conservative bodies, which allow them to expend less energy than the rest of us. But conservative or not, most of us do not have to live with the sword of Damocles—aka type 1 diabetes—poised above our heads.

. . .

AT THE CLOSING ceremonies of the BMWMOA Rally, a stunt plane did loops and dives above the assembled crowd. The plane flew straight up to become a fleck in the air, continuing to rise more and more slowly until it froze, nose heavenward. After interminable seconds, it pitched sideways, to start falling whence it had come. Faster and faster, until what appeared to be only feet separated it from a fiery embrace of the earth. Thousands gasped as one. But John Ryan and an Iron Butt pal of his were laughing, because Ryan had just commented, "Good thing *I* can't get a pilot's license." They were instantly visualizing the type of show he would put on—one that would make this look like a beginner's lesson.

Diabetics are prohibited from piloting aircraft due to the dangers of hypoglycemia, low blood glucose: rapid loss of coordination, altered perception, unconsciousness, and even death, if not treated promptly. (Other debilitating complications that can arise include blindness, kidney failure, nerve damage, and heart disease.) A medical dictionary advises: "Those with Type 1 diabetes must take special precautions before, during, and after intense physical activity or exercise." Ryan (first diagnosed with the disease as a teenager) faithfully monitors his glucose level, although he and his friends, and sometimes his doctors, are at odds over what constitutes proper treatment. After watching him take two plates of cake from the buffet line, then meter his blood so that he might take an appropriate amount of insulin to counteract their effect, one friend who happened to be a nurse got up from the table and, before storming off in disgust, announced to the table, "John Ryan is a noncompliant diabetic!" Other friends, notably his female ones, have discussed among themselves what they view as his particularly bad food choices. He is unduly fond of chocolate-covered Oreos, and he once phoned in excitement from a Whole Foods Market, with the ecstatic news that the store carried a bacon-chocolate bar. Yet other friends simply worry in silence.

• • •

I FINALLY get around to the question I had been fairly afraid to have answered. I have been thinking about it while the injured gas tank of my K75 drips its remaining fluid into a porcelain bowl, after a long day in which Ryan has been helping me reassemble the bike after I started the dominoes (and the tank) falling with an especially stupid move that shall go undescribed here, because it is simply too embarrassing. I want only to have my bike operable in these, the waning days of autumn, before I have to put it away for good, and then pine through the winter months for riding weather to return. We eat dinner, a fire going in the fireplace.

What happens if his blood sugar gets dangerously low while riding? Has it ever happened? I wait for the answer, at once apprehensive and eager.

Yes. He has blacked out and crashed, twice: once in 1995, and again in 2002, before he got an insulin pump and had to rely on injections.

For a moment, I am stunned—but I am also not at all surprised. I have to throw it off myself, my astonishment, so I decide for safety to cast it onto others. "And what would you say to people who would protest that you could kill yourself, or kill someone else, by continuing to ride?"*

A beat. Then an outburst of laughter: "I'd tell them to go fuck themselves!"

And suddenly it's the funniest thing I've heard in a long while, because of course it's absurd. *Could a little thing like that keep John Ryan from riding?*

\* \* \*

**ON NOVEMBER 14, 2009,** he phones, in as black a mood as I've ever heard him express. Discontent is chafing him like sand in the underpants. His bank account sank below a hundred dollars and they charged him a usurious fee. There are few to zero moneymaking prospects on his horizon; excited hope that a large check is in the offing from sponsorship proposals wars with the kind of realism

---

\* Of course, I know that occurrences of injury to anyone other than the rider in motorcycle accidents have always been statistically minuscule—soothing knowledge to everyone except bikers.

that only a half century on the planet can fit one with: he'll believe it when the money's in the bank. He is beginning to see, with his peculiar, prescient understanding, what will become evident within a few months: that the money is going to stay just where it is, which is everywhere but in his bank account.

Oh, and he had been shorted two pills by the Woodstock pharmacy near my house where we had gone to fill the phoned-in prescription for antibiotics when he finally admitted that the infected follicle on his hand—a white dot in a sea of inflamed and puffy flesh—was reminding him of the time, twenty-five years before, a similar thing had happened and a doctor started talking amputation; yet another side benefit of diabetes. He had paid more than fifty dollars out of pocket for those pills, and now a day's worth was missing.

Maybe the worst insult to his mood this night, though, was the advent of Thanksgiving. This prompted some of Ryan's usual sardonic invective of the four-letter sort. "I hate Thanksgiving!" he declared, with the same self-knowledge of his singularity in the midst of common contrary sentiment he evinced when saying, as he frequently did, "I hate children!" I think he did not. He just wanted both, the holiday and the small people, to be exactly as he wished them to be, only they persisted in being different. The idea of being forced to sit around a whole day with family, overeating, was pissing him off; it was not about riding, and that made it suck. "When I make a lot of money, I'm going to have Thanksgiving at my house. Only people who come on motorcycles are allowed." That was something he could look forward to, at least. "Some of the best Thanksgivings I ever had were spent alone, a microwaved burrito from 7-Eleven eaten on the beach." Of course, the memory vied with his intense desire for companionship, too, and he bemoaned the fact that "kids today" seemed no longer to view the night before Thanksgiving as one of the year's best nights to party, as when they used to fill the New York City clubs like Studio 54 and Xenon, and John Ryan would be among them. Then again, he was not a kid today. He was something different. And, as the years sped on, more and more detached from what he was, as were all of us: transformed.

Two days before Thanksgiving, he called again. His belligerence had, if possible, increased. Why did I not know this was blood sugar talking? It had taken his personality prisoner, just as it had another time when, on the phone, his speech became syrupy, his reasoning muddled, his ideas repetitious, and his ability to decide on anything, even what to say next, as substantial as vapor. One day before the holiday, I was in Ohio, and my phone again lit up with the name John Ryan. Only this time it was not Ryan. It was a close friend who was in New Jersey to celebrate Thanksgiving with the Ryan clan, using his phone to contact other close friends. He had discovered John in his room, unconscious, in a pool of vomit. No one knew how long he had been out, or why. It seemed likely that it was a diabetic seizure resulting from hypoglycemia. It is possible his numbers had been erratic for a while, which would explain the increasing hostility I had heard from him. (People who live with diabetics report that the most mild-mannered of people can become aggressive to the point of physical violence during episodes of low blood sugar.)

The next week I drive down to the hospital in Morristown, where I see John Ryan as I have never seen him before: weak, uncertain, alone.

He keeps asking me if he has any shoes in the room. He wants to get up and leave. Now. Waiting for word on his release, which I suspect will not be the one he wants, we go over recent events; he asks me about himself. I tell him things, to a look of befuddled interest, as if he is hearing about an acquaintance he vaguely recalls. Then we discuss Christmas, which he allows is a pretty good holiday, since people are nice to one another for about two weeks. And the other thing he likes about it? "When you find the perfect gift for somebody. That feels good."

He remembers that I own a K75, but he thinks it is burgundy. (It is blue.) He keeps asking the same questions, including how long I had been away from bikes before rediscovering them, though this one he can answer himself; apparently a span of eleven years without a motorcycle was confounding enough that it made an impression so deep not even global memory loss could erase it. He remembers that I have a son, and wonders who is watching him while I am here, but he cannot remember other things. He cannot remember what kind of bike he owns. He cannot remember that five months earlier, he rode from Alaska to Florida and broke the world record.

He is not certain of anything except that he wants to go home. He had found his way to the hospital's library and logged on to a computer to send two messages before he was discovered and escorted back to his room. He wanted to connect again, and he wanted to get out. He wanted to ride. His family had already impounded his bike, though; they knew him very well.

In a misguided belief that he is about to be released, he goes into the bathroom to inject some insulin into his gluteus maximus, a procedure just visible beyond the door he neglects to close fully. That is when a male nurse enters the room to see my worried, wondering expression. "Don't worry, honey. They get it back. They always get their memories back." I manage a small smile of relief. Then that meant he would ride again. No one knew how far, but he would ride again.

Later I will read from the Mayo Clinic that

*Left untreated, a diabetic coma can lead to*
- *permanent brain damage*
- *death.*

• • •

**RYAN'S CHRISTMAS GIFT** from his family was the keys to his FJR. He goes out for a ride immediately. The rear shock-absorber linkage needs to be replaced, however, and there are other serious matters. There is no money for them, and no money either to retrieve his old K75 from the mechanic who had been charged with replacing the wiring harness after it had fried itself from the demands placed on it by the many auxiliary systems required by a long-distance rider. Still, he retains hope: "The K75 will need a lot of work, but it may have a few long rides left in it." In January 2010, he looks to the one ray of light emanating from owning two used-up carcasses of motorcycles:

I can't complain much. If I had worked more and ridden less, like the hopeless millions out there, I might have some money in the bank, and it would take a lifetime to wear out a bike.

By mid-February, however, the urge to get going again, to be on the way to something big, the ever-longer rides that sustain him and give him purpose, is running hot. I ask how he's doing.

Extremely wonderful, thank you. I have a great view of my motorcycling life circling the drain.

. . . And, what else is there, really?

It is a question I cannot answer. Not anymore.

# 10. Only these rides

*We should not really be surprised to find so many forms of nomadic life. For much of human history—even in hominid times—we have evidence of populations surviving by movement.*

—NEVILLE DYSON-HUDSON, IN *NOMADS OF THE WORLD*

*We treat our future selves as if they were our children, spending most of the hours of most of our days constructing tomorrows that we hope will make them happy.*

—DANIEL GILBERT, *STUMBLING ON HAPPINESS*

**I AM WONDERING WHERE,** amid the bolts and cylinders and wires, they installed the sorcerer in the BMW K75. Twenty years ago, I had written that it was the only other bike that turned my head, in the way of a boy on the street who in a brief exchange of looks shakes you to your core and then passes on but leaves a faint scent hanging in the air: what might have been. Now I owned one. It had returned me to life. It returned me to physical aliveness, and it led me, thirsty, to the water of social connectedness. It spread before me new possibilities, many of which were realized. It also faced me with problems of control and confidence, which represented the reverse aliveness of needing to confront difficulties. There is no true joy without the necessity of learning where joy's edges are, the place you can fall off into the empty space of nonjoy. A K75 was going to return John Ryan to life, too, only a year after he had helped me find the one that opened me to feeling alive (and troubled) again.

The phone rang one night in April. It was a mutual friend calling to say he was on the verge of buying another K75—one for which he had neither money nor personal need, but one he felt compelled to buy even before he had concocted the excuse he would give to a very angry wife. He was going to buy it for himself, but first he would take it to Ryan's house and leave it there for him to ride until he could find the money to get his own back from the mechanic who had fixed it. He said he didn't know why he was doing this, only that he felt he had to. In the world of the peculiar logic that seemed to belong only to the K75, it was true. He had to.

By "giving" Ryan a bike, he was giving him more than a machine (it was always thus, it seemed, with motorcycles and the people who truly love them): he was giving him the chance to become again who he is. Starting small, certainly; starting imperfectly, for the K75 was no FJR. But starting again from where it all starts (again), the K75. He was giving himself something, too, although at the moment of the transaction, when the money left his hands, he doubted the benefit of a sudden kind act.

When Ryan finally did manage to gather the several hundred dollars to get his own bike back—in its own way also a hideous machine, beaten up and unbeautiful, as any bike ridden by John Ryan for some two hundred thousand miles necessarily will be—he was back on the road for real, on two wheels that were his. Still, it was not possible to see his large frame hunched over this relatively small, primitive vehicle and not feel bewildered. There was something of the comedown, and the slowing down—triggering a primal fear—in the sight. There was something of the mortal. Was this a motorcycle on which he could contemplate fourteen back-to-back Bun Burner Golds, or a record run from Alaska to Tierra del Fuego? Perhaps. There was no mention of when, or how—now anyway. The big-funds man had disappeared a few months earlier, back into his big-funds world, a place for which the renegade rider was ill-fitted.

When I returned home at night after a ride, the driveway, the garage, seemed like a dark maw into which I might fully disappear if I were not careful. Unable to describe a tight-enough circle to position the bike at the door, I stopped at the head of the drive to use the small incline to roll the K75 backward while I sat on it. At the lip of the garage, I would dismount, carefully, willfully, leaving the sidestand down just in case. Of course, this meant I could not let it lean one whit, or I would risk catching it on the concrete seam and visiting on myself the small disaster that I was working to avoid. Then I would heave it backward, using my calf on the foot peg to push, while saying silently, "I *will* do this. I *will* do this." After it was on the centerstand, my muscles were shaking and my forehead glistened with sweat. At least it hadn't gone down, to where I could not get it up again.

In the mornings, I repeatedly watched a video of police motorcycle maneuvers while hoisting small barbells over my head, and later I talked endlessly with other motorcyclists, some of whom had a hard time visualizing my difficulties and told me I just needed to practice; others told me it was quite plain that I needed a smaller motorcycle. (The gift Lario was still in the hands of the good elves who were rehabilitating it after its many seasons of disuse with its previous owner; even when restored, I was told, it would be my "show bike," not the one on which to light out to far ends of the map. Its outsize charisma had always been counterpoised against certain limitations of reliability, as I well knew.) I followed all the advice, to a point, sometimes going to an empty lot where I was just as afraid to tighten the circle as I was out on the street. There was a wall in my brain where the will to flow should have been, and the order of procedure—weight to outside peg; push on inside grip; stay in the friction zone and trail brake; turn head *all the way around!*—stopped in the middle like a broken tape. Wait—now, which is first, which next . . . by which time I was through and had ridden five feet outside the box. If the painted lines had been curbs, I would have been on the ground with a very heavy bike on top of me. Despair settled in. And that is when I started to think that the others—the ones who had advised getting another motorcycle—had a point.

The same nauseating remorse one feels when tasting the thought of breaking up with a lover began to fill my mouth. All the places the blue K75 had taken me came back, the thousands of miles, one after another: Tennessee, my SaddleSore, the frozen ride to Florida, the Berkshires, the Blue Ridge Parkway. This seemed a betrayal. Long-distance riders, in particular, cannot help but personify the machines with which they partner for such long and difficult feats. "I've never had any problems with the tranny," one might say—and then, immediately: "Oh, god, I hope I haven't jinxed it now." In other words, it is an omniscient (and mischievous) spirit that hears things through garage walls. And in its heart lies a perverse will of its own.

You know the motorcycle is but a machine: it can't think, feel, or infer. It is outside any value system. It is a tool—like a lathe, a dishwasher, the family car, a computer (which is far more complex). Yet everything in the rider militates against believing this. The act

of riding imbues the bike with a spirit: the time spent with it is cre-
ationary, so that the key in the ignition is the active equivalent of
Michelangelo's God reaching out to Adam and with one electrical
spark calling forth all of human existence. (Go ahead, tell a rider his
bike doesn't make decisions, know right from wrong, teach lessons,
give gifts; go ahead, tell me that the sight of the waters of the Hud-
son literally dancing with light at the touch of the slanting sun as I
passed over it on the bridge today, in a dark mood full of forebodings
of an ending, was not in fact redemptively given by my motorcycle
at the moment I most required it.) You spend more time with your
computer, may depend on it for everything from a livelihood to a
means of communication with others, but you're never going to feel
that it has a soul. Souls are the province of motorcycles alone among
machines.

I now went out to the K75 wearing the same sidelong look I
might have shown a boyfriend I was thinking of replacing: hoping
it couldn't see into my thoughts and dump me first. Someone had
mentioned that an R1150R might be a good fit for me. I went to ride
one in Virginia, and it felt thrilling: balanced, light (though it was
almost as heavy as the K75, the center of gravity was back down low
where I'd always thought it belonged), the brakes highly effective
but not grabby. The next month, I located one for sale in Kentucky
with only six thousand miles on it—practically new. I enlisted John
Ryan to fly there and ride it back: eight hundred miles, so he would
be back in another day.

The K75 went up for sale. For weeks its picture graced listings
on several sites. No one inquired. It was a seventeen-year-old bike
with lasting powers, which meant there were many others just like
it out there. One night, just when I thought there might not be any
hope, I received a message: "I was not looking for a bike. I was look-

ing for a new car. But somehow I saw yours. And I have been toying with the idea of returning to riding after a long hiatus. The K75 is exactly what I had envisioned as my comeback bike." It turned out the man lived just over the mountain from me. He came over the next day. And the day after that, with cash. Then it was gone.

· · ·

THERE ARE ONLY these chances. The ones before you. There are only these rides, the ones you set out on. As the years wound on, around the axis of me, something changed. There was an understanding, falling peacefully on my shoulders like snow, that there was a finality, and that finality was a grace given. It permitted appreciation of what you had without the burden of *more*—always, and ever, more to come. There would not be.

A weekend was set for the Lario to be delivered. The core group of fixers, who had labored for months, and who now wore T-shirts bearing a picture of the bike with the legend THE MAGNIFICENT SEVEN on one side and PROJECT LARIO on the other, would bring it from New England so it could occasion a party, some photos, and a ride—the usual run of events where Moto Guzzis are concerned.

It was brought to the park pavilion, where a large meal was also being prepared, amid joking and music. I looked at it parked there, its sinuous lines both familiar and strange (*is this really mine? have seventeen years been erased by fiat of some kindly god?*), and a sense of unreality came over me. I doubted I was worthy of this moment. I feared I was going to have to say something. And what could I say that could even touch the gratitude I felt? I almost wished it had not happened. I know how this sounds. But it was beginning to feel unbearable. I walked over to the edge of the lake and felt utterly alone, again.

But even a good cry can't last forever. The mastermind, the chief genie, came to stand beside me. His presence there was enough. He knew exactly what this meant; after all, he had chosen to place Moto Guzzis firmly in the middle of *his* existence, too. Then it was time to ride.

The next morning, the Lario was in my driveway, and several people were crouched around it, pointing. There was something amiss, and that is when I knew it was finally back, and not a dream at all. It was well and truly my Guzzi. At last they located it: a short caused by a loose fuse I never would have found, even with a voltmeter, which I have now been instructed on how to use but may never truly understand. In the words of the song, some things will never change.

I approached the triumphant group. I now knew what I wanted to say: that I had been struggling, mightily, with what to say, but I could not find the words because there were none for an act this large. They had restored not just a motorcycle but a heart.

* * *

**POSSIBLY NO CLAIM** is in fact too grandiose to make about motorcycles, because they are infinitely expandable. They change lives, and they give life as well as take it away. Only now can I be as piercingly aware of this as I am. Before, I might have found Andy Goldfine's belief that riding on a daily basis is a social good—outlined in his introduction to what I believe to be the most important book ever written on the subject, Steven L. Thompson's *Bodies in Motion* (and hinted at in the pages of Goldfine's Aerostich catalog, with its equipment for the rider who is far more than a hobbyist)—a bit outlandish. This idea is original to Goldfine, and (I see now with my latter-day eyes) it is also complex and, finally, true. As he sees it, "Even the most mundane riding experience changes the rider in psychobiological ways which ultimately are beneficial to everyone." This is because riding makes one proficient in all sorts of things (including risk management), and a proficient person is a better member of his community. He cites the "episodes of transcendence" that riding provides—the beautiful and inimitable sensation of being two disparate things at once: very relaxed and very alert. "When we ride motorcycles, we decide to be idealists."

He understands that the communal job of making life safer is what drew hominids together and enabled us to evolve to our current level of sophistication—along the way adding the creation of religion, the social fabric, larger brains and all the incredible stuff they are responsible for making, and finally the natural craving for yet more of those human-originating experiences of managed difficulty. *These make us feel alive because they are what made us.* This is why motorcycling is so important.

I closed Thompson's book, my own besotted thinking validated (family and friends chalked up the silly smile I frequently wore to a temporary infatuation; one acquaintance, annoyed with my sudden inability to write on any other subject but motorcycling, sent a petulant yet true message: "Just because motorcycles are almost everything, doesn't mean they are absolutely everything"). Then I continued thinking about motorcycles.

The experience of riding is primarily aesthetic: we become artists when we ride, a combination of dancer, painter (in air), sculptor (making three-dimensional shapes). And if the originating purpose of art was as adornment that would attract mates (as well as tell wishful narratives of survival, as in cave painting), then this primitive impulse is present in our compelling desire to get on a *pretty* bike and ride. But the desire to ride is overdetermined, too, as are the most important things about the most complex animals that ever roamed the planet: it is both a way to become better at all the things that make us peculiarly human and a way to express to others where we rank (another important means of improving chances in the competition for mates).

Aagh. I get one "aha" moment after another, until finally my head is hurting the same way it did in a college philosophy course when I briefly, just for one second, grabbed hold of what Jacques Derrida actually meant. Then it flew away again, a milkweed spore on a September wind. *Come back!*

More and more, spiraling down, opening up. It goes on forever. That's what motorcycling is like, if you think about it for very long.

• • •

**THE MOST FRIGHTENING** thing man has ever attempted, I feel certain, is that walk between two buildings on a thin wire, nothing underneath but a dangerous amount of air. When I read Philippe Petit's words now, I see an image of someone who might or might not be John Ryan, riding through the darkness of night, away, far. "I am curious of everything. I enjoy life. I know that life is short and life is beautiful, and therefore I don't risk my life. That surprises people, because they think I have a death wish. But no. Actually I've got a life wish."

• • •

**AT SOME POINT,** I start getting huffy at people raising a "theoretical," "just for interest, you know" question that is clearly directed at what is beating behind my very specific, slightly freckled chest. "You will have to answer the question of *why people take this much risk,* especially, say, people with young children." Oh, do you possibly mean "people so much like me they *are* me"? A simple question wants a simple answer, aphorismlike. So I drive over to the secondhand shop to pick up something, and I find a line by Helen Keller: "Avoiding danger is no safer in the long run than outright exposure. The fearful are caught as often as the bold." How about the danger to my son of living with a perennially pale, soppy mother? Better to have an animated one joyous for a brief while than to be saddled with the weight of an unhappy presence in the house for extended years. Just as a dead body seems impossibly heavier than a live one, so does a dead soul to the loved ones forced to haul it around to family events.

I received the gift of knowing my riding seasons are numbered, and now I see the paper in which it's wrapped is reusable, too. If I waited until my child was grown and on his own, I could have a two-wheeled ride all right: an aluminum walker with wheels.

A lot of people think it insane, our riding long distances for no other reason than a voice—heard in the head, or in the gut—that tells us to. Then again, sitting in front of the TV eating Cheetos is insane, too.

• • •

**THE "PIZZA PARTY"** in Jacksonville in March 2010, at which no pizza was served, was the first official gathering after his Ultimate Coast to Coast where John Ryan could be saluted by the people who matter most to him, his peers in the Iron Butt Association. We were supposed to have ridden there together; I spent the day before I left chipping a path through that ice on my driveway. Then I rode to New Jersey, where I was supposed to have a new rear tire mounted that he had ordered from his local shop. Only he had forgotten it. Forgetting things had never previously been part of Ryan's approach to life: he collected all stray bits that floated down his canal and built a watertight ship from them. He told a seminar room full of listeners at a rally about how he attacked the UCC ride. He had no doubts he would accomplish it, even after three setbacks; part of his preparation was mapping every single twenty-four-hour gas station along his route. His planning skills are aided by his natural tendencies, including what he claims to be a near-absence of circadian rhythm; he cited an entire week once spent at Daytona during which he slept only six hours. He also told the audience that during his record ride he didn't take off his boots for four days, an act he warned brought predictable results: "People aren't going to want to socialize with you," which got a big laugh.*

The next morning, when we were scheduled to leave New Jersey, Ryan paused to do anything and everything except leave: tend to his sister's horses; run an errand in the truck. When I finally felt pressed to depart for the shop that had a tire for me, in order to avoid riding all night, he couldn't start the BMW GS he had borrowed from a friend. I made my way through a dark sleet outside Washington, DC, and soon pulled in to a Holiday Inn to thaw out overnight, arriving in Jacksonville the next evening. We kept in touch by phone. Every call ended the same: *Still at home. Can't get this damned bike started.*

In the morning, I looked in the mirror and recoiled. It was clear I no longer bounced back like I once did; such are the wages of age. Get used to it. Get breakfast.

As I entered the back door of the lobby in Jacksonville and aimed myself toward the dining room, my eye was drawn to some activity on the other side of the glass doors at the main entrance. The exact

---

* He ended by telling the audience, "It is strange and humbling what this ride has done, and what people think of it."

replica of John Ryan, distinctive Aerostich and all, was dismounting from a GS. But no, this *was* John, with his impossible *I-have-done-what-few-mortal-men-can-do, so-what-are-you-looking-at?* bearing. He inclined his head to pull off a black helmet covered with stickers. I knew that one of them read: "If I have to understand don't bother to explain," in an inversion of the common dullard's claim: "If I have to explain it you wouldn't understand." A short time before I was falling backward onto an anonymous print bedspread in a riding-induced stupor in Florida, he had managed to get the engine to light up. It had leaked so much fuel over his left leg during the fifteen-hour ride, covering 929 miles, that the dining-room staff took aside a patron at the table where Ryan had just taken a seat and asked him to "kindly remove that man" from the room. Instead, Ryan reluctantly removed the suit and put it outside with the bike.

In the Ramada banquet hall that evening, the epicenter of motorcycling distilled to its essence, empty coffee cups and dessert plates littered the white-clothed round tables as the assembled riders stopped their chattering. Mike Kneebone took the podium. He talked about the "Legends" of the association (when you begin archiving your history, it occurred to me, a certain level of ossification has been attained), around whom a group SaddleSore had been organized the day before: Bob Higdon; Dave McQueeney ("one million six hundred thousand miles of sick and twisted rides"); Ardys Kellerman; Jim Owen, winner of the 2009 rally, whose first documented Iron Butt ride was New York to San Francisco in less than fifty hours; Shane Smith (four Iron Butt Rally Top Ten finishes, including a win in 2005); Marty Leir, winner of the 2007 rally; Ross (winner of the third running of the rally) and Jean Copas. He presented certificates to all who had just finished their first Saddle-Sores, and welcomed them into the association.

Next he pulled out another certificate and held it up for all to see—even though they couldn't, the room was so large. They knew what it said, in recognition of an incredible eighty-six hours and thirty-one minutes for a ride of 5,645 miles. "We have our secret clubs," he intoned, "and you, John Ryan, will forever be in the secret UCC club." As Ryan moved to leave his seat to receive his due, Kneebone started tearing the certificate into tiny bits that fell like snow to the floor. He then reached down to pull out another, this one saying only, "under four days," a mathematical vagueness.* Ryan, who had retreated, now got up again and this time took hold of an acknowledgment, in the only form the Iron Butt Association would give. Those who knew the rest of the story, the one that would remain written only in wind on the slate of the memory, stood up in a body to give Ryan, standing by the podium with a shy, proud smile, a standing ovation. A moment of effusion, and then they sat down.

Standing around with beers in hand after the ceremony, chattering resumed, a number of Ryan's colleagues remarked on how subdued he appeared. I could point to no single factor; certainly, since he had gotten out of the hospital, he seemed slowed, like a 45 played at 33⅓, frequently struggling to remember things, telling the same stories over and over. As usual, too many possibilities crowded into my mind: the aggravation of a malfunctioning motorcycle; the continuing frustration of not being able to make things happen when and how he wanted. But I think the biggest was being here, with his tribe, without *his bike*, his badge, truly his "better half." This

---

* He also qualified for a Bun Burner Gold, 1,678 miles in "less than" twenty-four hours (actually, an unpublished twenty-one hours), which he accomplished on the first day of the ride.

is what that term really means, I decide. He looks like a man who has lost something.

One of Ryan's friends, an unusually determined rider himself, said flatly, "He shouldn't be on a bike." This community sympathized, but it did not mourn. Hell, these were people who were so itchy they could barely say good-bye; all of a sudden they would stand up, say, "Well, I gotta go," and *go* they would. You'd run into them at the next event, thirty or forty thousand miles down the road. "A tough nut to crack," observed another rider of the standard personality type in the IBA.

Mourning requires standing immobilized for a time; that is its nature. These are movers. Whether they are running from something or to it, that is up for interpretation. In the manifold way of all human existence, it is probably some of both. Similarly, I would offer the possibility of a dynamic between these divergent motivations for the extreme ride, given by two long-distance motorcyclists themselves: One believes it is a symptom rather than a cause; the other thinks vice versa. I may simply be unable to choose, but a dynamic moves, after all, so it is especially fitting. But one thing is readily apparent about the group as whole: Its behavior is as steeply codified as that of the Knights of the Round Table, and it is not just people playing dress-up with swords and copies of *The Romance of the Rose*; it is serious, because it is life-and-death played with motorcycles on real roads. The code of behavior is unwritten, but transgressors will be put out in the freezing night, their rights stripped as surely as if they were clothes, and left to die in the elements. An outsider, a long-distance neophyte, who posted to the LDRider list about his deep dismay that at the 2009 rally finishers' banquet there was no formal acknowledgment of the fact that Davo Jones was lying near death in a nearby hospital was treated to such terrific hostility and lambasting (one sin among others was his neglect to check before he wrote to see whether a fund for the family had been started, which of course it had been) that in effect he was summarily shot by firing squad. Reading the replies left me shaking. *("Do not embarrass this organization!")*

As far as John Ryan went, he was lauded, he was one of them, he was extraordinary, but even he had to get out of the way when it was time for others to go. It was *sauve qui peut* in this group. His ride was in the past. They would give him another standing ovation, maybe, when he got on with it. And if he didn't ride on from here— more, farther—well then, they would.

· · ·

BY THE TIME the New York bike show rolls around again in January 2010, I simply cannot believe it's been one year since I met this man. In that year, he has managed to change my life utterly. I have a motorcycle because of him; I have ridden about six thousand miles in (or near) his presence. I know the look of his unlined face, every aspect of its expression. I have seen him in most states on the Eastern Seaboard, talked to him countless hours on the phone. I have thought long about him, written about him, talked and corresponded with others about him. Just a year! Just a year for everything to change.

And did I know him? No. There is no way to truly know one whose response to almost anything was to ride away. Two epigraphs vied in my head as right for a chapter titled "John Ryan." Which should it be?

*When people see a strong horse and a weak horse, by nature they will like the strong horse.*

Psychologically astute of Osama bin Laden, I think. I wonder if he had ever met John Ryan.

*Show me a hero and I will write you a tragedy.*

For one so young, F. Scott Fitzgerald was able to cut astonishingly deep into human truth with a single slicing look.

Both of these came to mind as ideal, although they diverged completely.

For one so difficult to see into, for one doing such difficult things, a lone epigraph was not enough, as it would be for anyone else. So two it would be.

• • •

**DR. KEITH USISKIN** was Ryan's endocrinologist a decade ago. His voice on the telephone is gentle and kind, and Ryan said the two enjoyed an excellent relationship as doctor and patient. This is not the case with his current doctor, whose guidelines on treatment, if followed, he maintains, would not permit him to ride long distance. So Ryan does not follow them. Life simplified.

When informed of what happened to his former patient the previous November, Dr. Usiskin let out a sigh of dismay. These things happen, he said, though with less frequency these days. In the past ten years, there have been advances, with new insulins and with the pump, which allows for better controlled delivery.

He admired Ryan's fortitude and appreciated his good-humored approach to his illness as well as life in general. However, he said, "I was always nervous about the motorcycle. But he was committed to them; it was his essence. We couldn't take it away from him. I never would have encouraged him to attempt that extreme ride, though."

It was clear he did not know the half of what his patient did on a regular basis in the saddle.

On the question of a full recovery from the seizure, Dr. Usiskin paused. "Well, it is true that at fifty the body finds it harder. But with will and determination . . ." He seemed unwilling to allow himself to think that Ryan would not make it all the way back. And indeed, if, medically speaking, will and determination were factors in the regeneration of neurological and motor capacity, no question remained on the subject of a complete return of powers in this case. Within a year, in fact, Ryan was displaying fewer and fewer lapses in short-term memory, which had seemed the harder hit. Life would continue to enliven things with its bold ironies, too: the Thanksgiving after a friend had found him insensible on the floor of his bedroom, Ryan was hundreds of miles from home, nursing the friend through his own difficult illness. For the better part of a year, he lived in temporary residence with him, tending to every need of a sick man. With little opportunity to ride during this time, his dogged pursuit of excellence had no other outlet than Facebook; the status update had rarely known such creative ardor.

Yet the intervening year, which brought him closer to whole, also brought him closer to the end, as I was keenly aware. At what point does the body simply say, *I can't do what you ask, what you live for.*

The reason Dr. Usiskin and John Ryan got on so well, it became obvious to me, was that both were durable optimists. Asked to comment on the projected lifespan of those with diabetes, the doctor again paused. "Our knowledge is based on older literature," he said. Yes, but what did it say? Pressed, he confessed, "The data suggest it will not be normal."

Nothing about John Ryan was normal. Why should this be any different? It made sense and sadness both.

• • •

**FOR ALMOST TWO** years out of my ever-shorter lifespan, too, I felt nothing. I'm not saying I had no emotions; I had altogether too many of those. But I *felt* nothing, for my senses had no object on which to practice. No touch, no exhilaration; I existed in a place far from sensations, excised away. Sensations are the clock of *now*—and *now*, the Buddhists tell us, is life. So when motorcycling gave me sensation again in abundance, it also gave me life.

I rediscovered the deep pleasure, for instance, in economy, in seeing how far I could reduce what I needed.

Can you make a satisfying dinner out of the three odd items in your refrigerator (syrup, carrots, an egg)? Can you take to the road with everything you need strapped to the bike?

After traveling with Ryan once or twice, I found I lost my affection for what I once felt represented the epitome of primitive economy: no sit-down meals on a trip, not even fast food, but, rather, a cellophane-wrapped bagel or a pack of peanuts from the gas station, eaten while sitting on a curb next to the bike. (Apparently the latter was a long-favored meal substitute, since a friend recalled for me a forgotten episode from post-college life when I met him one night during one or another romantic crack-up, slapped a packet of peanuts on the bar, and uttered only one word: "Dinner.")

Now, in a further pleasant economy, I was getting fond of what seemed almost complete self-sufficiency, with peanut-butter-and-jelly sandwiches, trail mix, and water bottles packed in the bags and eaten standing. Stretch while you eat: no use wasting all that time to sit down on the curb.

I could never, however, go quite as far as John Ryan and eat salmon straight from the pouch, eschewing fork and, more important, mayonnaise. His horoscope for September 17, 2009, mentioned the need to overcome "pathological levels of self-sufficiency" and ask for help. I suspect this was not offered in regard to food, however.

So many new pleasures to be had in my new life: not only a second life as a motorcyclist, but a second life as fully aware that its end was rushing toward me with great velocity. I corresponded with motorcyclists from all over the world now, thanks to the medium of the computer, through which they easily located me. Even at that disembodied distance, or maybe because of it, they knew me mysteriously well. Or maybe they just knew motorcycles. "I'm glad you're back riding," one of them wrote. "I believe the motorcycle found you in your time of need."

• • •

I THINK ABOUT what it must have been like two hundred years ago, five hundred, a thousand—with no great invention like the two-wheeled conveyance that has become something like a need for so many, the story that fills hours and imaginations, the thing that brings *such joy*. There was nothing for the men of yore. Their weekends were empty.

Maybe humans—or some portion of them, anyway—have in them something that draws them inexorably to habit, to addiction. I am reluctant to stop *anything* once I start, including proceeding down what I know is the wrong trail, or mowing the lawn when it's too hot to do so. We don't like change; the next chapter we read could be the end.

I suspect that long-distance riding has something to do with viewing myself as immortal: it is a picture I have of myself in my mind, and I should be embarrassed to describe it, standing slightly up on the pegs, riding down the highway, relieving the stress of this long in the saddle—doing so precisely in order to spend more time in the saddle. If I ride on, well, then I'll ride on.

Sometimes, though, between the delight and the denial, I look down into a crack and see the sadness there. I am sad for him; I am sad for me. I am sad for all of us who have something we love this much, something we love most strongly for its temporal nature, and that is precisely what is going to take it away. In that sense, there is never enough time to ride. So we try to make the ride last longer. We are motorcyclists all, trying to outrace time's wingèd chariot—and who, in the end, has more horsepower to the rear wheel?

I realize, with a start, what this book is about. Death. Not motorcycling, but death. Or, rather, motorcycles as life force and death force at once: the game played so we can safely approach the end, in which one side is squashed by the other. That is when the buzzer sounds. We get up out of our coffins and clap each other on the back. Then we go for a beer.

How else to look at black finality other than to toy with it? Let us laugh! No, first we fear (inchoately, so we do not feel) and then we deny. We embrace as we push away. We ride intensely, almost stupidly, to the edge, and then we recoil from what we see far below in the abyss. There's no way to process this, except by proxy.

I wondered whether another FJR danced persistently out of reach of the man who could ride the hell out of one because failure was not an option. Overnight, the end became just visible, a mote in the eye. I was beginning to be bothered by a subtle change in my vision, too—and it was not only the dollar-store reading glasses I now had to hide, like contraband, in every room of the house.

Every ride has the structure of music. A theme emerges, then the refrain. In between, there will be a bridge; there will come variations. The tonality, the key, and the tempo are created of the weather, of vibrations, the slant of the sun, the corners, the chip seal or the tar snakes or the new paving. Finally there is a coda. See, in every piece, whether concerto, hymn, or opera, there is beginning, middle, end. This is invariable. Some rides contain melodies you have never heard before. They are in a minor key, and they haunt. Because they are strange, they recur later to you, when at rest. In the sound is combined all the rides you have taken and all the rides you will never make. There is in the air an elegiac tone. These are the rides that, far off, sound just like a requiem.

# Afterword: *There Is Only Forward*

**THE ICE ON THE DRIVEWAY** was a glacier in miniature, my very own science exhibit demonstrating what happens in polar regions when the temperature remains above freezing for even a few days: the ice retreats. It shrinks. It goes back up into the sky. In the American Northeast, what felt like it was never going to come was in fact early in February 2011.

The first springlike day causes the sap to rise. In the trees too, maybe. But I mean the sense, in most motorcyclists, that something wonderful is about to happen, that some gift is about to arrive. And indeed it is.

John Ryan has never been prone to this seasonal anticipation, this pacing in the waiting room of the birthing center. The petty distinctions between winter and summer, riding season and Battery Tender time, have never been his. But the winter of 2010–2011 was not riding as usual for him; it was not spent riding at all. He was still quietly engaged in what he had been doing since late summer: taking care of a sick friend. He had largely abandoned the K75, a well-loved but ugly beast with the fuel cell he had used back in the days of his first long-distance records strapped onto a platform he had lately fashioned for it out of Trex composite decking (strong but light; his own idea). The bike looked like someone had taken a scouring pad to it but had never finished the job of cleaning it. The bike was still smoothly and perfectly tuned, though, eminently rideable but yet not ridden. That is because, in his role as caretaker, he simply had to use that vehicle universally derided by motorcyclists as a cage, a system of constraint for both the body and the soul. Not that he was resigned to it: he groused openly online about having to drive "in one of those evil four-wheel fuggers." But he did not and would not complain about giving up the defining center of his life. Only a few of his closest compatriots knew what he was doing, or why, or where. That in moving hundreds of miles from home to see to a fellow motorcyclist, for however long he was needed, he was doing something that few others could, or would, do for anyone, even a blood relative. That he was in fact doing something unprecedented, and in such a way, heroic. Once again.

Meanwhile, John Ryan was waiting. He was waiting for another FJR to appear, somehow. He was waiting to take another far, far ride. And he was simply waiting, as we all are waiting.

He did not know when the time would come, only that an arrival or a departure eventually would take place. He did not know whether the air rushing past his ears would be caused by the beating wings of the white angel or the black one. Just as no one knows. Yet we wait to go.

When the story is finished in some as-yet-unknowable future, it will form a parable. About perseverance, or motorcycles, or life. (After all, they are pretty much the same thing.) It ends, like everything, farther down the road. There is no going back. There is only forward.

# Acknowledgments

**MOTORCYCLISTS** may be strange, but they are never strangers. I have been the recipient of almost breathtaking generosity and assistance from many, many of them, simply because I, too, ride. And/or was working on a book on their favorite subject. I feel preemptive dismay at forgetting any one of them in this accounting, but it is almost a given with my partly operational memory. Forgive me (again). Those whose help and friendship I greatly appreciate include Bob Hower, Adam Novitt, Michele Bissonnette, Craig Bennett (the angel of the K75, among other things), Andrew Garn, John Leffler, Jim Shaw, Ed Milich, Claye Curtis, Tina Hollaender of Motolights, Sam Booth, Paul and Voni Glaves, Greg Hertel, John Shields, Carol Yuorski (aka Skert), David Nash, Reid Dalland, Kevin Gillen, Ed Allyn, and Bill Shaw.

The inordinate kindness of a special few exceeds even that of those above; these are MaryJo Gracin, Doug Jacobs, Charles Statman, and Peter Jones—the elegant writer and racer whose imaginative generosity to both John Ryan and myself has literally changed everything.

The entire Iron Butt Association has my gratitude, especially (of course) Mike Kneebone; also Lisa Landry and Ira Agins. Bob Higdon gets his own category, he's that big. Not only would I probably never have met John Ryan were it not for him—you're responsible for everything, Bob!—but his philosopher's (and humorist's) insight into the long-distance enterprise informed nearly everything I've written here. In addition, he read my book in manuscript form, even though the time was inconvenient for him, in order to correct a galaxy's worth of errors.

The IBA website was a much-used tool for research (as was the *Iron Butt Magazine*, edited by Bill Shaw), especially the ride reports, notably those of Chris Sakala and Bob Lilley. I am indebted as well to beer, in its function as lubricant for getting lots of great stories out of IBA members at various gatherings.

The brotherhood of Guzzisti once more proved the bond of something thicker than blood. I will never be able to say how deeply I have been touched by the kindness of the members of the New England Guzzi group, so many of whom contributed to restoring my faith, and a beautiful silver Lario. Special mention goes to the Magnificent Seven: Tom Halchuk (chief genie), Bud Clauer, Tim Fiehler, Sean Ryder, Doug and Jacqui Ritchie, John Chicoine, and Scott Reichert. Scott has his own compartment in my heart for being who he is: the best.

I thank Dr. Keith Usiskin for sharing his medical insight, and John Ryan's sister and brother-in-law, Sue and Dave Drillock, for their hospitality on numerous occasions.

My agent, Betsy Lerner, is the kind of fierce champion every writer deserves but few have. There is no way to truly thank Amy Cherry, my incomparable editor; she knows when to cut and when to hold, and she is a good friend as well as the most trusted literary adviser I could ever hope for. Her assistant, Laura Romain, is both supercompetent and helpful.

David Drummond is the Designer Who Would Stop at Nothing; his jacket design is an icon of stylish subtlety. Appreciation also to my panel of advisers on design: Lee Harrington, Jacky Davis, Lynn McCarty, and Janet Harrington, friends all.

I trust it has not escaped notice the measure in which I admire John Ryan. Those lucky enough to call him friend know the most loyal and rewarding companionship possible in this life. He is an artist of his chosen metier, and it has been an honor to watch him at work. He gives everything he does a hundred and forty percent, and access to his life, thoughts, and dreams was made no exception for a writer hopelessly in his debt. Thank you, John, for never giving up—on me, or on going the distance.

A few individuals deserve my deep gratitude for helping get me through a dark passage and into the light. Paramount among them are Kim Hunter, Beatrice Weinberger, Lynn McCarty, Carol Meyer, Sally Eckhoff, Jolanta Benal, and Valerie Turrens. Once I was there, Mark Friedman made it beautiful and bright. Thank you more than you know.

My son, Raphael, is to me, every day, a wonderment and a joy. He is also a cheerful and game pillion. He, too, will take his own long ride and amaze us all. That is why this book, and all my love, is dedicated to him.